Muriel L. Hine

Simply
PRECIOUS

Moments in Time
with a
Remarkable Cat

by
Muriel L. Hine

Printed in the United States of America.
ISBN 0-9651188-0-0

Published by Muriel L. Hine
1075 Watervliet Shaker Road
Albany, NY 12205
Telephone 518 456-4214

Book and cover design by Griffith Publishing,
Caldwell, Idaho

DEDICATION

This book is dedicated to every individual who has ever been privileged to be owned by a fur-covered friend.

To everyone who has ever given food, shelter and love to an animal.

To those dedicated to the cause against cruelty to animals, who have searched crowded streets, fields and woods to extend a loving hand to our defenseless, abandoned friends. God's love shines upon you.

To Muriel, "The Little One." I may soar like the eagle, but you have always been the wind beneath my wings. Without your love for animals, and your continued moral and financial support, this publication would not be possible.

To Precious, just for being.

Last but foremost—

To God for His very special gift of the little bundle of fur called simply, PRECIOUS.

I'm eternally grateful to each and everyone of you.

THANK YOU FOR YOUR SUPPORT.

This is a self-published manuscript, thanks to the financial assistance of Muriel Kinney. Any profit realized from the sale of this book will be donated by Ms. Kinney and the author to continue the fight for animals' well-being everywhere. You will receive confirmation of your purchase for tax purposes.

"A true friend is someone who takes you in when the rest of the world has cast you out."
—*Author Unknown*

Contents

Introduction

People everywhere ask, "Where did you acquire this beautiful, sweet, well-behaved cat with such an appropriate name?"

I always answer, "Precious is a gift from God to Muriel Kinney and me. She wandered over miles of rugged heavily wooded terrain, across acres of open fields, and forded a mountain stream before she stumbled onto the front porch of our house nestled in that wilderness."

A new acquaintance pointed a finger at me and remarked, "Wait a minute. I thought *your* name was Muriel."

I chuckled. "We share the same first name. Two Muriels. Friends affectionately refer to Muriel Kinney as 'The Little One.'"

The man stood there looking at the two of us. Muriel, a petite blonde, was overshadowed by my tall, heavy frame. He was still puzzled. "Never mind how the cat found your doorstep. What were you doing in that wilderness? Were you camping, hunting—what?"

A reasonable question. It happened like this.

In 1960 my husband Irving and my friend, business partner and housemate Muriel Kinney and I bought an abandoned 70-acre farm in Eagle Bridge, New York, to develop and operate a working youth camp and resort. We planned to do the carpentry work on weekends and vacations. We had built two homes so felt confident in the success of this building venture.

The first building to be constructed was for the main lodge and our living quarters. The massive 5,000 square foot structure was barely enclosed when Irv became terminally ill and died. Muriel and I made every effort to sell the property, but without success. We offered to give it to various organizations who worked with troubled youth if they would use the property for a youth camp. No one was interested unless we completed the building. Mustering all our courage, strength, determination and skills while shedding much sweat and many tears, we two women completed the lodge four years after my husband's untimely death.

By then so much of ourselves had gone into the project—physically, financially and spiritually—that we couldn't bear to part with the place. We sold our house in Albany, New York, and moved to our mountain. We believe it was God's will that brought us to that special place, just as it was a miracle that Precious found her way to our front porch on that cold October morning in 1980.

Simply Precious is more than just an animal story. It is actually an account of three living creatures—two human, one a stray female feline—who, for fifteen years have traveled together down life's road forming a bond that knows no bounds. As you turn these pages, remember that this could be the story of any one of the millions of animals who never get the chance to share their love and lives with others. I hope you enjoy reading about the life and times of this truly remarkable cat called simply, Precious. The book may make you laugh, bring tears to your eyes or stir memories of your own beloved pets. Precious has not only turned our lives upside down; she's touched the hearts of everyone she met. I'm certain she'll tug at your heartstrings, too.

THE UNINVITED HOUSE GUEST

D rive carefully and have a good day," I called to my housemate, Muriel Kinney, as she left to go to her office in Albany. I usually made the fifty-mile trip with her, but I was on vacation. She stuck her head out of the car window. "You be careful if you get on the ladder. And try to stay out of trouble today, will you?" She chuckled as she pulled out of the driveway and disappeared down the dirt road. Trouble? What trouble could I possibly get into? My computer consulting business was slow, so I had taken a few weeks off to do some work around the house. Today I would stain the carriage house.

I stood in the driveway admiring Mother Nature's artistry. The surrounding miles of woodland and open fields were ablaze with color. Shades of red, orange and yellow blended in with the stately evergreens, white birch and sturdy oak. Goldenrod and wild flowers of the field formed a frame for this masterpiece. The sun's early rays focused on the open field to the south, sending steam vapors skyward from the frosty crusted grass. The red beacon light on the air traffic tower in the Berkshires, forty miles away, flickered through thin morning fog.

It was going to be a beautiful day. I'd best get started. I had forgotten to empty the water pail under the front yard faucet the night before. Ice pushed above the rim of the bucket. While chopping the ice I glanced towards the open front porch.

Underneath one of the wood porch chairs was something black. A rag glove—a ski hat or maybe an animal. Skunks and porcupines were plentiful in our area. Cautiously I moved closer. It was an animal. I didn't want to frighten it, especially if it was a skunk. That would put me in enough trouble for one day.

No head was visible, but whatever it was, it didn't move. It lay shivering in the cold October air. I carefully lifted the Adirondack chair, the animal's only protection from the weather. The fur mass was a black and white cat. A black head with white outlined ears and white face struggled to turn towards me.

The mouth opened to cry out, but no sound came out. A pair of runny infected eyes pleaded for help. Long black fur was matted in layers. The white bib and chest hairs were separated by clumps of mud clinging to every strand. I removed my old red windbreaker, put it around the trembling body and carried it inside.

Two other felines, Minnie and Lover, barreled out the front door as it opened. They were anxious to begin their daily frolic and wouldn't return until dusk.

The four remaining housecats were already snug in their own private hiding places. Little Phella, Willie, Little Eva and Snowshoes never had the desire to go outside to explore the vast world around them. They were afraid of their own shadows and didn't like humans, either. The only time they showed their faces was at feeding time.

Each gave a look of "Leave me alone. I'll call you if I need you."

The warmth of the house seemed to stimulate the shivering animal—or was it the savory aroma of beef stew bubbling in the pot on the back of the kitchen stove? I set cooled broth down in front of the cat. The cat's legs weren't strong enough to hold its weight. The body flopped over on its side. The cat stuck its face into the dish and began to suck. It apparently felt good to eat. About half of the liquid disappeared. I wiped the tiny face and eyes with a paper towel and warm water. Exhausted, the cat curled down into the red jacket and went to sleep.

It would be another hour before the veterinarian's office opened. When I reached him, Dr. Aaronson said, "I'm sorry. I can't take the stray off your hands just yet. I have thirty cats I must find homes for. Can you keep it for a couple of weeks?"

"Sure, but it needs medical attention. I'm afraid to take a chance with the rest of my brood."

"I'll take a look at it and see what we have. Can you come right away? I have to leave for Rutland in an hour."

"I'll be there," I told him and hung up.

What was I saying? I didn't even know if this cat would ride. Cats normally hate automobiles except to get next to the warm motor in the winter. I'd just have to take that chance. I didn't want to use my cat carrier in case the cat had something contagious. I scooped up the red bundle, put it on the front seat of my Scout and took off.

We made the ten-mile trip without incident. The cat was probably too weak to rebel. Dr. Aaronson met me at the door, quickly took the bundle from my arms and disappeared into the examining room. After what seemed an eternity he emerged with the red jacket nestled against his two-hundred-pound frame. His head of short cropped sandy hair just cleared the doorway. His boyish freckled face was firm but pleasant as he quietly explained her condition.

"She's suffering from multiple ailments. The infection can be treated, but she's almost dead from starvation. I can treat her but I don't have anyone here to watch her awhile I'm away. She's very weak and will need a lot of TLC. Even then, I don't know if she will respond. Could you take her and keep her isolated from your other cats? I don't think there is any danger, but it's better to be safe." He struck a match to his pipe. "How on earth did she find her way to your place?" he asked. "You're in the middle of nowhere up there on your mountain."

His words circled around my head and came back to rest on the word "she."

"It's a girl?" I blubbered. I never could tell about cats. "I don't know where she came from. We're miles from the main road. She had to come over the mountain and across our stream. There is no way of getting around that stream." I shook my head. "I-I don't honestly know. She just appeared out of nowhere."

The doctor stroked the cat's head and ears while she stayed perfectly still in his arms. He dug into his white lab coat pocket and pulled out envelopes, bottles and an eye dropper.

"Here," he said, handing me the conglomeration. "Follow directions starting tonight. Meanwhile try to get some more broth down her. In between pills and liquid medicine give her small quantities of broth. If she responds, increase food gradually. Don't overfeed her. Her system must adjust. This cat's going to require a lot of attention. Even then I'm not sure she'll make it." Hesitating he added, "Muriel, if you don't want to mother this cat or don't have time, it might be best to put her down now while I've got her here."

My eyes dripped tears. I swallowed hard and asked, "What do you honestly think? Is there any chance of her surviving?"

He quickly responded. "If I possibly could, I would

put forth the effort. I only wish I could devote the time she needs to help her through this." He looked away then down at the cat. "I can give her the medical attention she needs," he explained, "but this animal needs more than that. Pets do better where they are in a home environment."

"But she won't be home," I remarked.

"You're right in a way," he replied, "but I have a gut feeling about this little girl." He smiled at the red jacket, gently jiggled the bundle before glancing my way. "If anyone can pull her through this, you can."

I hoped the doctor wasn't giving me a snow job. I was willing to spend the time—if it would do any good.

I put the red bundle down on the front seat of the Scout and walked around the other side. "Call me if there is any change for the worse," Dr. Aaronson said. "We won't let her suffer. I'll call you when I can take her off your hands"—a quizzical smile crossed his face—"unless you decide to keep her."

I shook my head. "One more animal and I'll lose my happy home."

The doctor knew exactly what I was referring to. Over the years, I had latched on to many animals. I was always bringing home strays and injured animals of every description. We once shared our lives with fourteen cats, five dogs, a three-legged opossum and two raccoons.

Muriel put her foot down. "NO more—Don't you dare even pet a dog unless it's wearing a collar with a license."

I put the medicine on the back seat and headed for home. The cat remained in the Scout until I had time to fix a place for her in a spare bedroom.

Muriel's reaction to the sick cat was as expected. "You know we can't keep this animal," she steamed while viewing the critically ill patient. "You promised."

"I know, I know," I said, "but I'm only going to try to

nurse it back to good health so Dr. Aaronson can take it in a couple of weeks."

"A couple of weeks? You're expecting a miracle?"

She looked at me, the cat and back to me while shaking her head in a hopeless fashion. "OK—as long as you remember we agreed there would be no more animals. With our busy schedules there just isn't enough time, and it isn't fair to the animals not to be able to spend quality time with them."

She started towards her bedroom to change clothes, mumbling, "What about all the work you planned for your vacation? I don't see any stain on the carriage house."

The bedroom door slammed behind her. I stood in the hallway talking to the door. "Our present brood of animals don't care. Their definition of quality time is a full bowl of food, a warm place to sleep, the freedom to be left completely alone. There is still plenty of time to finish my list of chores."

The nursing process had begun. One-half pill every six hours starting 6 p.m. Liquid medicine every six hours—starting at 9 p.m. Feeding between pills with the eye dropper around the clock. Every hour and a half the alarm sounded. I was so groggy it took me several seconds to remember why the alarm was ringing.

I made a schedule. When I told the doctor I had time, I didn't realize it would turn into a twenty-four hour a day job. So be it. I had made a commitment to this animal and I would see it through to the end. My chores would just have to wait.

Four days into this ordeal my housemate sent a questioning glance at the cat and me. "Any signs of improvement?" she asked.

I shook my head. Muriel was compassionate even as she began her lecture. She knew I was committed to this animal.

"You're carrying garment bags under your eyes," she

said. "How long do you think you can keep this up?"

I fought back the tears. "She's fighting so hard to survive. I can't give up on her yet. She is taking in more food each time I feed her. Look."

I pushed the chart in front of my concerned friend. "If she doesn't show signs of improvement by Monday I'll take her to Aaronson."

I was so choked with emotion and exhaustion I couldn't continue.

"Clang! Clang!" The alarm went off. It was time to push the pink liquid into the fragile, feverish open mouth. Muriel went on to work, leaving me with my nursing chores. The patient was cooperative. She made no attempt to free herself from my grip as I slipped the eye dropper into her mouth. She sucked the end like a kid sucks a lollipop. I wondered why the medicine hadn't started to show some effects. I called Dr. Aaronson.

"Give her a few more days," he told me. "Try mixing a little canned food with the broth to form a soupy consistency. Don't overfeed her, though. Her stomach has to get used to it."

His voice, soothing and caring as always, filled with hope and concern. He tried to comfort my weary mind and body. "Continue the medication," he ordered. "I gave you enough for two weeks. Call me either way on Monday."

The driver from the bottle gas company was pounding on the front door while I was on the telephone. Ralph usually made my house his first stop when I was scheduled for a gas fill-up. He always took time to have coffee and home-baked muffins or Danish. I had been rocking the cat ever since Muriel had left early that morning. The cat was still in my arms.

"What the devil happened to you?" he blurted. "You look like you've been run over by a truck." Ralph was never known for his finesse. Before I could squeeze in a

---

"good morning," he pulled the red jacket down from around the cat's body and exclaimed, "What is this miserable looking thing? Good God, woman. Do yourself and the animal a favor and have the vet put you both out of your misery. This pathetic looking creature will never make it. Trust me."

He gave me a scolding look as he poured himself a mug of coffee and plopped down on a kitchen chair. His hand reached for a blueberry muffin. Buttons on his coveralls strained, indicating he should pass on the muffin. His bright orange hat swung back and forth on the clothes peg where he had tossed it. The morning sun caught the specks of silver in his coal black heavy mop of hair, emphasizing the character lines in his weather-beaten face.

"Darlin', you're a good cook," he mused as another muffin disappeared. For a moment I enjoyed the flattery, but the spell was soon broken by the sound of the alarm. Ralph jumped, spilling coffee from his mug. "What in blazes was that?" he yelled.

"Time for the cat's medicine," I answered. Ralph sat down again, shaking his head, his mouth stuffed with food. A swallow of coffee freed him to talk.

"If it isn't squirrels, opossums or raccoons, it's any stray that comes along. What's with you anyway? You can't be Mother Theresa to every wayward animal or creature that happens along. Nature has its own way of taking care of these things. This cat doesn't have a chance. It's best you get rid of it before it kills you."

I could feel my face redden. The cat made no fuss when I pushed the pill in her mouth and rubbed her throat until she swallowed. The diversion gave me time to cool off. Ralph was one of the few people I allowed to hunt our seventy acres which bordered state lands. He showed great respect for other people's property and for the wildlife he hunted for food. I really didn't want to hurt his feelings by spouting off at the mouth. However, the pressures of the past few days caught up with me.

"Ralph," I said, "I know you mean well. You're one of the most caring and sensitive people I've met since moving to this mountain. But doesn't every living creature have the right to life? I don't share your viewpoint about hunting, but at least you hunt to put food on your table."

I grabbed the coffee pot and poured. I felt a sudden urge to get on my soap box. I pranced around the kitchen table, holding the red bundle and started my retaliations.

"It's amazing. Civilization is riding Eddington's great arrow of time. We are enthralled with high technology, conquering new frontiers, crusading for people's rights for this or that. Unfortunately, while we cling to that arrow roaring towards the twenty-first century, the values of human resources, self-respect and decency seem to have gone astray." I came up for air, then submerged back into my speech. "We live in a throwaway society. Everything from paper plates to lives. Crime is on a rampage." I picked up yesterday's newspaper and slammed it down in front of him, pointing to the front page headlines— "CHILDREN MOWED DOWN IN SCHOOL YARD!" I said, "Children are being killed on streets and in school yards. Drugs are of epidemic proportions. Women and children are being battered. Animals that humans have the nerve to call their pets are being abused and abandoned by the millions."

Ralph hadn't moved a muscle since I started. He finally interrupted me. "Hey! Hey! Wait a minute. I'm on your side. I'm one of the good guys. Remember?" He got up from the table, walked to my side and put a muscular arm around me. "Take it easy. I know how deeply you care for your animals, but this little tyke doesn't have a chance. I'd hate to see you get down sick because of it." He spun me around to face him. "What would I do for breakfast when I come up on this mountain?" A broad smile crept over his face.

We both sat down. He poured more coffee. Tears rolled off my chin onto the red jacket. I mumbled, "You're right, Ralph. You usually are. I'm sorry I took my frustrations out on you. It aggravates me so to see poor defenseless animals being used for human pleasures, and then cast aside like an old shoe or yesterday's newspaper. What did this poor little thing do that she doesn't deserve a chance to live?" I was looking at the cat in my arms. Tears continued to roll.

Ralph handed me a napkin and told me to blow my nose. Two muffins went into a plastic bag as he grabbed his hat and started out the door. He poked his smile back inside. "Take care of yourself, will ya? I'll call in a couple of days to see how you're doing."

The alarm clock sounded as Ralph pulled out of the driveway. He had spent over an hour with me. I couldn't remember—was it time for medication or feeding? I was so distraught I barely knew who I was.

I mixed a little canned food with the broth. I put the cat down in front of the food. Her front legs crumbled beneath her. Her rear end stuck high above the rest of her body as if ready to pounce on some demon that might lurk around the bedpost. She swallowed hard, then gagged. I added more liquid to the mixture. That went down easier. I took her in my arms, wiped her mouth and eyes with a napkin, sat down and began to rock. Feverish eyes stared up at me, then closed. I burst into tears and prayed for God's help. Still rocking, I must have dozed off. The next thing I heard was the alarm.

Monday morning I mechanically dialed Dr. Aaronson's office fearing what he might tell me. He was ecstatic when I reported the cat's intake of food.

"Great!" he yelled into my ear. "Once she starts eating I think the medicine will stand a better chance. The poor little thing was so near death from starvation she had nothing to fight with. It may take a while before her fever breaks. We still have this week. Hang in there. I know you can make it happen."

(Yeah Doc—still polishing the old apple, huh.)

The days ticked away. It was Saturday again. The cat was standing on wobbly sea legs, but managed to eat without toppling over. She still had a fever, and her body shivered.

Muriel gave the cat her medicine before coming into the kitchen with me.

"I want you to go stretch out for awhile. You're falling in your tracks. I'll mind the alarm clock."

She took hold of my arm and directed me towards my bedroom.

I balked. "I can't. The cat may need me."

Muriel pointed to the bedroom and snapped her fingers with an accompanying order. "Go! I'll watch the cat. If you'll feel better, I'll put the cat along side of you on the bed, but you must get some rest. I insist."

I fought back like a kid but finally gave in. Muriel wrapped the cat in the freshly washed red jacket and put her down next to my right arm. The cat didn't move. I stroked its head and dropped into a deep sleep.

I was aroused by a tickling around my face. A pesky fly no doubt. My hand went up to brush it away. I heard Muriel's voice whisper, "Easy. Someone wants to say hello."

I opened my eyes and looked straight into the eyes of the cat. Over the last four hours she had rallied, gotten up and come up by my chin. Her long whiskers were touching my face as she tried to wash. I sat up and took the animal in my arms. The embrace was so intense the cat let out a grunt.

Muriel joined us on the bed. Tears of joy flowed like water. My eyes glanced upward while my mouth mimed— "Thank you, God."

Simply Precious

By the time all of the medicine had been used, the cat was able to walk and eat solid foods. Another problem surfaced. She had no control of her kidneys. There was a trace of blood in the urine, too. Her rectum was still raw, despite ointment applications.

I thought, "Dear God—don't tell me that this poor thing has gone through all these painful days for nothing."

Dr. Aaronson declared the cat to be on the mend, but should continue to take the prescribed medicine. "I think she'll overcome the blood in the urine."

Further examination determined there was something wrong with the cat's hind legs. There was no flexibility in them. This explained the humped back when she tried to lie down.

"We'll take x-rays when she gets stronger," the doctor said. Seizing a bunch of matted fur in his fingers he said, "Try to get rid of this. It will make her feel better. And put a little Vaseline on her rectum. See you in two weeks."

The cat's health improved daily. After each medication I held her on my lap and tried to remove the clumps of dirty tangled gobs of fur. A brush and comb didn't budge the matted mess. Scissors were the final solution. Snip-cut-brush. Snip-cut-comb. She looked like a kid who grabbed his mom's scissors and started to clip his own head, leaving gouges and irregular clumps. She was bald in some spots, but there were no more tangles.

The cat was a good sport during this entire ordeal. I was sure she'd rebel with all the combing, pulling and tugging, but she never moved. She stayed perfectly still while I did my handywork. In fact, the day I groomed her bib and stomach, her head nudged my hand when I stopped. She wanted more.

It was easy to fuss over this little sweetheart. She was so loving and had the most gentle disposition—so unlike my other rabble-rousers, who wouldn't let me within five feet of them.

My hands were brown with dirt from the cat's fur. She needed a bath. I looked in our animal medicine chest. There were more things there than in the human one. I picked up the dry shampoo bottle, read the directions and checked with her doctor before attempting to tackle that thankless job. Dr. Aaronson saw no reason why a light dry shampoo would hurt. He warned me, however, "Cats don't like baths. If she won't cooperate, don't force her. I can give her a bath when she comes in for her x-rays."

This little ragamuffin took to grooming like a duck takes to water. She loved it. She stretched out on the sheet and allowed me to do anything I wanted to. I had to turn her body from one position to another. To my surprise, there were no fleas, ticks or ear mites. Her toenails were so long they curled under. Four days later the makeover was completed—including a manicure, nail polish and a pink ribbon around her neck.

The rest of my brood weren't even remotely curious as to what was going on behind the closed bedroom door. Their routine remained the same. Breakfast at six-thirty. After breakfast Minnie and Lover went outside, and the others retreated to their favorite hiding places. Lover's favorite spot inside was in the living room on the wide window sill behind the Boston fern. Minnie always curled up on the rug in front of the fireplace in the studio. The sick cat was still confined to the spare bedroom. She hadn't met the rest of the clan yet.

On November 18 Dr. Aaronson took x-rays of the stray. He looked bewildered when he brought the cat out of the examining room. He slid the x-rays under the light. They showed a scar around the middle of the stomach. Both hind legs were pinned with metal rods or pins. "This cat has suffered a dramatic accident. Probably hit by a car.

Simply Precious

Whoever had her spent considerable money on her—four or five hundred dollars at least. She's been spayed, too. I'd guess she's about fifteen to twenty months old. Chances are she jumped from a car window on Route 22 near Cambridge. The owner may be looking for her." He buried his face into the fur and kissed the white curly stomach.

"What do we do now?" I asked.

"People sometimes check in with animal hospitals when they lose a pet. I haven't had any inquiries, but you might ask the vets in Hoosick Falls, Cambridge area. Also check the bulletin boards at the Grand Union and A & P. This cat has been well taken care of. I'm sure somebody's looking for her." He handed me the bundle of fur, smiling. "You might even get a reward."

I only half smiled back. "I'd like to find the owner, but no amount of money could compensate for what this cat and I have been through these past weeks."

We placed an ad in the local paper, but there were no responses. Dr. Aaronson asked me to keep the cat until after Thanksgiving. She was such an adorable, docile sweet thing, someone was sure to want her for Christmas—that is, unless I wanted to keep her. My response was the same as before. "No."

Our road had a steady stream of traffic during deer hunting season. The idiots who called themselves hunters shot at anything that moved. Our property bordered thousands of acres of state land.

Our land was posted, but that didn't stop them. Bullets whizzed overhead from all directions. One farmer raised goats and painted GOAT on their sides with whitewash so they wouldn't accidentally be shot. A thoroughbred Morgan horse was killed on the other side of the ridge. The hunter told the forest ranger he thought it was a deer. That thought cost him thousands of dollars.

I never took chances with my animals. Minnie and

Lover were unhappy campers about it, but they were confined to the house during hunting season.

I let the stray cat out of the bedroom, leaving her free to roam the house with the other four-legged inhabitants. Her presence had no effect on the older cats. They simply ignored her, and she was too busy following me around to care.

Every year Muriel and I hosted Thanksgiving dinner for about thirty people. The guests lived alone, most were elderly, but all were good friends. Some of the men went hunting during the early morning hours, dragging themselves back to the house in time for dinner. As soon as the first guest arrived, the six older felines scattered. Upstairs, downstairs, behind the piano. They wouldn't be seen or heard from again until the last stranger left.

The stray cat, on the other hand, was at the front door before either Muriel or I could open it. Her runny nose and eyes were now clear. Her black head was accented with white trim around each ear. A sweet white face that could melt a heart took shape directly beneath two massive yellow eyes and a pink nose. Long whiskers stretched beyond a ruffled white bib. On the underside of her chin was a big blob of black. A small black beauty mark near her right nostril completed her portrait. Unfortunately, the rest of the body looked like an unmade bed with a moth-eaten cover. Gouges here, holes there. Long strands of black fur hit and missed on her tail. One hind leg sported a beautiful fluffy black and white pantaloon. The other one had no fur at all.

The little ragamuffin showed no signs of feeling conspicuous. With her bottle brush tail standing high, she greeted each person coming through the front door. Moving slowly, she escorted each guest into the living room—stopped and looked back like a maitre d' to make sure they were following. Once the individual was seated, she returned to her post in the front hall to meet the next person to arrive.

Simply Precious

Everyone wanted to know where the cat came from and what had happened to her fur. Guests commented, "Isn't she just the sweetest thing you ever saw? She's just precious."

Like grandmas with their grandchildren, pets dominated the conversation for most of the day. Everyone agreed, this stray cat was something else. No one had ever seen anything like her. So friendly, loving and attentive. One cat owner readily admitted, "This is a first for me. My cats won't let me anywhere near them." She wasn't aware that our six older cats were playing hide and seek elsewhere in the house.

The last guest to leave wasn't out of the driveway before the unsociable felines were in the kitchen begging for their dinner. All nine house occupants were soon stuffed with turkey and all the trimmings. Minnie settled down on her rug in front of the open fire. Lover found his way between the flower pots on the window sill. Snowshoes decided to be sociable and jumped up on the television set. Banging of swinging doors going upstairs indicated the other three people haters were settling in for the night. I picked up the little four-legged hostess and went to a rocking chair. She never moved but looked into my face, purring her contentment.

The following Saturday the dreaded call came from the veterinarian. He had found the perfect home for the cat. Could I bring her over right away? Silently, I went down stairs where Muriel was doing laundry. The cat followed. Brump-Brump—her hind legs not bending.

My lips drooped and when I told my housemate the news, Muriel's eyebrows narrowed, her face tightened. "You're going to give this cat away—just like that?"

I threw her a quizzical stare and stammered, "Y-Yes. You told me I couldn't keep any more animals. Remember?"

The cat expressed her opinion by rubbing against

my leg and uttering a quiet "Iow, iow." My heart pounded in my ears. "He said they were nice caring people."

Muriel threw a towel back into the dryer and scooped the cat up in her arms. "How could you even think of such a thing? After all the two of you have gone through together." She paced back and forth in the laundry room. "I swear, I don't understand you some times. You can't give this little girl away. She adores you. You'd break her heart." She took a deep breath and kissed the cat. "You call Aaronson and tell him this precious little thing has a home. Ours!" She shooed me with her hand. "Well—don't Just stand there. Go!"

I headed upstairs. The cat tried to wiggle from Muriel's arms to follow. She followed me everywhere—even to the bathroom. I could hear Muriel's voice saying, "It's all right, sweety. Your mommie isn't going any place. Neither are you. You mean too much to both of us. I guess you're stuck with us—Precious."

My steps quickened. My heart was full as I made the call. My refusal to relinquish the cat came as no surprise to the doctor. Dr. Aaronson's soft, understanding words still ring in my ear.

"I told the Hatfields not to get their hopes up. You and the cat have gone through so much together. I'm glad. I don't think you'll ever regret it. There's something magical about that little girl. She's a sweetheart. Simply precious."

I thanked him for everything and hung up. Muriel was still holding the cat when I returned to the laundry room. Tears of joy flowed from both of us. The cat was baffled, obviously thinking something was terribly wrong. She nudged Muriel, reached out and kissed me on the nose. I smothered her with kisses, looked into her big yellow eyes and whispered, "Welcome to the family."

Muriel beamed ear to ear. In unison we sing-songed "Precious."

Thus began our journey together and the name of Precious for our newest family member. I was elated. I nearly squeezed the breath out of Muriel while I yelled, "Thank you—thank you!"

My housemate shrugged her shoulders. "What's one more cat?" she said, and went back to her laundry. Precious followed me to the kitchen.

Dr. Aaronson was right. There was something magical about this cat. We didn't know how this little bundle of love would change my life completely, as well as spread an abundance of joy to others throughout the years that followed. Nothing would ever be quite the same again.

ON TOP OF MOUNT THOM

Country living isn't for everyone. Many city dwellers prefer the hustle and bustle of the asphalt jungle. Some wouldn't even visit such a remote area. Muriel and I chose to live on our mountain.

The only drawback was the commute to our offices in Albany, fifty miles away. I was more fortunate than Muriel. I did free-lance computer conversion of manual accounting systems. Much of my work could be done at home. Muriel was administrator for a large printing company in Albany. She had to be in her office every working day.

I was often joshed about living in the woods. "Well, what did Daniel Boone and Mingo do this weekend?" were among the comments thrown at me on Monday mornings. As much as they ribbed me about being a stump jumper, some of my acquaintances asked if they could come up to our camp for a day or weekend of roughing it.

They envisioned a small log cabin or slab wood sided cottage, no running water, no lights, with a wood stove and an outhouse. Not so.

What our house guests saw was a massive gray-tan structure, which I referred to as a battleship in dry-dock, sporting black shutters, a manicured three-acre lawn, flower beds and shrubs, tastefully landscaped, complete with swimming pool. A forty-mile view stared back from the south. The only other things visible were stone wall fences and trees. Acres and acres of maple, ash, oak, pine and white birch.

Inside, hand-hewn beams, pegged pine floors, genuine wood knotty pine walls and battenboard doors enhanced the warmth of the colonial decor. There was no hand water pump and no outside privy. Three bathrooms, strategically placed, accommodated our guests. Every conceivable electrical appliance lined the kitchen walls. This was Precious's new home.

Good weather had all but vanished, leaving my THINGS TO DO LIST with more than half the items still unfinished. When Muriel remarked, "What's one more cat?" she didn't realize this "one more cat" would be completely different from the rest of our pets.

My few weeks of vacation stretched into two months. Terry, my office assistant, handled the everyday things with ease, but I knew I had to get back to work.

The first snow storm of the season dropped two feet of the white stuff. All felines were housebound. We didn't know what to expect when we turned the key in the front door after a long day.

The first day away from the house didn't show any change in house activities of our cats. Precious jibber-jabbered while following me around, but I thought it was because she had missed me. The other fur-covered residents continued to ignore the latest addition to the family.

Precious didn't take the snub lightly. She pranced around, made strange noises—none of which I understood. Occasionally she'd swat towards cats as they passed, only to be flattened by the exchange of blows. No fancy pants with a fat bushy tail, wearing pantaloons was going to invade their territory or tell them what to do. Oh, how wrong they were. . .

Training with Precious wasn't easy. Precious was smart enough. *I* was the problem. I couldn't decipher what she was trying to tell me. I was familiar with cats letting out with a MEOW and nothing more. Not this feline. It was as though she spoke a different language. Many Canadians traveled through our area. Perhaps her former family spoke French.

She never said, "Meow." At first I wondered if the cat had something wrong with her voice box and couldn't form the letter "M." I learned that her vocabulary is far more extensive than that of any other feline I've ever known. As you read the vocabulary list please note each one carefully, where the emphasis is placed, and any actions that she might make.

VOCABULARY LIST

Iow	This sounds like" I love you—we're friends"
Eiow	"I'm here and need attention."
<u>E</u>iow	"You're not paying attention. I'm getting impatient." Pacing usually accompanies this word.
EIOW	With a combination of jumps up your

---

	leg indicates something is wrong. "You better get your butt in gear and follow me."
Eeo	She hangs the "o" like a question. She wants to know if I'm all right.
EEO	Is a panic word when she can't find me.
Eiow	She rolls the "w," which means "I'm hungry." She also heads for the food closet or paces back and forth in front of the stove.
ERRO	"Don't argue with me. This is an order. DO IT!"
RROW	This is a growl. Notice she leaves off the "E" and "I." It is a distress signal. May day-Mayday! Come quick. Somebody's in trouble. Follow me..."

Now you know why it took me so long to understand.

This young, innocent-looking creature must have been trained as a guard cat and graduated to the rank of drill sergeant. She was a tough cookie. Even I felt sorry for the rest of the brood.

The first order of discipline was proper care of the bathroom. Once Precious was allowed the freedom to roam the entire house, she didn't relinquish her own private bath. She detests dirty litter pans and refuses to go potty if the pan isn't clean.

She's polite—"Eiow, eiow." If I don't snap to it, she starts her song and dance—"Eiow, Eiow." If that doesn't do it she lets out with "EIOW, EIOW!"

Once, in a fit of anger, I yelled back, "If you're so fussy, why don't you learn to use the toilet like some cats do?"

She responded with a disgusted look that indicated she preferred not to be compared to a Siamese.

The drill sergeant also inspected the bathrooms used by the other fur-covered residents. The two males never bothered to finish covering up. (Like men who leave the toilet seat up.) "ERRO, ERRO!" echoed from the powder room. Vigorous scratching with more reprimands followed. The rest room inspector cornered the sloppy user up against the wall, behind the litter pan. While "ERROs" flew, Willie braced himself for the worse.

For weeks afterwards, there was no privacy for Willie when he went to the bathroom. Precious followed him in and waited to make sure the message had been received. Even I lost my corporal stripes for a few days when I didn't clean the litter soon enough to suit the inspector.

Anyone who shares his life with a cat knows that cats will never stay on the floor. Not as long as there's a chair, table, stand or anything else they can spring to and from. You wonder if the floor's dirty, so you scrub and wax it. Before the wax is dry the cat is all tangled up in it. Then you hear the sound of someone being sick from licking the sticky substance from its feet. The cat gives you the look—"See, that's why I don't use floors."

Precious must have had excellent training as a kitten. She never jumps on furniture unless invited. She had a fit when she saw our aerialists use the end table for a spring board. To her, these felines resembled birds soaring through the air. Her drill sergeant's instinct surfaced. "ERRO. ERRO. Don't even think about it. You belong on the floor."

In short order, the troops scurried to their favorite perches slipping and sliding in their haste to reach their destination before the inspector could catch them.

She tried to keep them from shelves, window sills and off the TV set, but I drew the line there. I explained to her that these places were sacred to those who occupied them, and that it was all right. She grumbled her disapproval, paraded around, offered her last word before she settled down on her cushion, on the floor.

For years I had been dubbed a workaholic. I never knew enough to leave the office and go hone. When I finally pulled myself away, I had an arm full of homework with me. This changed when Precious arrived. I felt the urgency to get home—mostly to see what this cat had been up to during my absence. She was always at the door to greet me. At night she curled up on my papers while I mapped out diagrams, flow charts and testing examples.

The shut-ins did not like spending the winter indoors. We came home one night to find Lover swinging on top of the wagon wheel light fixture on the ceiling of the dining room. Precious was on the floor beneath bellowing, "ERRO, ERRO!"

The first warm day in spring Minnie and Lover wanted out—anything to get away from the inhibited months they had endured.

I had mixed emotions about letting Precious outside. I didn't know how she'd react. She showed no signs of wanting to follow Minnie and Lover. She preferred being with me, under my feet whenever possible. Every time I went out the front door a piercing "EEO, EEO" came from inside.

One weekend in early spring, Muriel and I decided it was time Precious was reintroduced to the wide, wide world. Ten yards of top soil dumped on the north lawn the previous fall had to be spread. (One of the THINGS TO DO that didn't get done.) I went to the tool shed for the wheelbarrow, shovel and rake. Porcupines had chewed the handles on the tools. Instead of having the wood for dinner, I wished they had learned to use these tools and given me a hand.

I set Precious down on the pile of soil. We fully expected her to scamper off across the lawn. She just sat there. "Iow, iow."

We took a minute, scratched her ears while talking to her. "Mommie and Muriel have to move this pile of dirt. Are you going to be good and stay home?"

"Iow, iow."

"We love you too," I whispered in her ear. Precious dug in the dirt pile while I loaded the wheelbarrow for Muriel to wheel and dump. Muriel started across the yard. The cat looked up from her digging and began to run.

"Here she comes," I yelled. "Try to head her off so she doesn't get into the woods."

Muriel dropped the load of dirt and started running towards the cat. Precious scooted around her, but instead of running off into the thicket, she jumped into the middle of the wheelbarrow. For the next four hours Precious waited at the big dirt pile where I shoveled, then hopped on top of the load and rode it like a cowboy training a bucking bull to its destination. It took only three trips for the cat to figure out how to shift her weight in order to stay on.

That night when Minnie and Lover came in for dinner, they looked around to see if the sergeant was gun-

---

ning for then. A sense of relief poured over them when they saw Precious stretched out on her cushion—sound asleep. She'd had a hard day.

Tension between the animals gradually subsided. Precious was too busy helping with chores to be bothered with the activities of the other fur-covered residents, although she continued to monitor the litter pans and made sure everyone stayed on the floor when commuting within the house.

There wasn't a task too big for this five-pound bundle of fur to tackle. She was in the middle of everything Muriel and I were involved in.

It was good to see green grass push up after a heavy blanket of snow. The riding mower started on the first turn of the key. Servicing the mower was one thing I did get finished the previous fall. The noise didn't phase this little curiosity seeker. She bounded after Muriel, so close we thought she would get caught by the blade. "No!" isn't in this cat's vocabulary. Our little helper was grounded until cutting was finished. The mournful sound "EEO, EEO!" penetrated the walls. Something had to be done before next cutting.

I fastened a wire bicycle basket to the front of the mower. I tucked the old red jacket, now hers, inside before raising the cat into the mower's crow's nest.

The fearless sea captain surveyed the waves of tasseled grass while bouncing to and fro as the mower bounded over mounds made by moles and into ruts washed by winter's snow melt. She diligently saw cutting to its end, never moving, then sauntered into the flower bed and took a nap.

It was impossible to do anything without this feline tagging along after me—like little brothers or sisters with their elder siblings. There was always work to be done around the house. I gathered tools, materials and supplies in a bucket and started my climb up the ladder onto the out building's flat roof in need of repair. (Another THINGS TO DO.)

My left foot was on the roof when I heard, "RROW, RROW!" below me. Precious had started up the ladder after me. Both front paws were wrapped around the fourth rung, the rest of her body dangling in the breeze. She could have let go and gone to the ground, but she didn't. The S.O.S. cry continued.

I shoved the bucket onto the roof and scampered down the ladder to rescue my furry friend. Her unfortunate experience didn't discourage her. She insisted on being on the roof with me.

Another five-gallon pail was retrieved from the shed. The fur ball sat in the bucket. I grabbed the handle and climbed to the roof. Precious surveyed her bearings and remained well away from the edge of the flat surface. I troweled tar. She concentrated on the maple tree branches overhanging the east corner of the shed. I pushed the trowel into the tar bucket while I went to see what this cat found so interesting.

A family of robins occupied the crotch of the branch. Inside the nest were four open mouths. Mommie and Daddy took turns feeding their young. In-out. In-out. They didn't seem to mind they had an audience. Precious made no effort to go after the birds.

We both sat on the roof, motionless, watching. It was three o'clock before I realized I had been bird watching for two hours. Tar completely covered the

---

trowel handle by the time I retrieved it.

Muriel wanted to know if there was a problem with the roof. When I told her what had happened, she snickered. "You? Sit for two hours? You can't even sit for two minutes. I'm going to have to talk to that cat. She's ruining your reputation."

The tar job should have been a one-day chore. It took three. Up and down the ladder, my passenger secured in her own private elevator. I concluded that my lay worker friend had much to learn about roofing. She was eager to learn, but I don't know who wore more tar—the roof—the cat—or me. I put the ladder up against the building a few weeks later. Precious went to her observation post but immediately returned to me. The young birds were gone.

Over the summer months I found myself wanting to stay home rather than make that hundred-mile trip every day. I brought mounds of work home, worked nights, leaving days open whenever possible to share with my furry friend.

Terry, my office assistant, was to be married in October. She volunteered to train someone and be on call if needed. That was more than fair, although no one would ever be able to replace Terry. She was like a daughter to me.

My office lease would expire September. Did I really want to keep my office in Albany?

"Terry, have you ever stirred in the early morning hours to the call of a Whip-o-will? Been lulled to sleep by the murmur of a babbling brook—a warm summer breeze pushing the scent of new mown grass through the window? Have you ever heard a symphony of crickets, katydids and tree toads serenade you—the hoot owl and bull frog chiming in at just the right moment?"

The young lady answered with a frowned brow. "I think so, once or twice at your place. Never paid much attention. What's that got to do with me breaking someone in for my job?"

"Well, these treasures have been mine, but I never actually heard those little chatterboxes, sounds and smells until Precious came to me. I've begun to appreciate the beauty and quiet of our wilderness. I think I'll close my office and work from home."

Terry didn't seem surprised. "If I lived where you do, I'd never leave. It's so peaceful and beautiful. I feel so relaxed after spending a weekend at your place."

Precious was sitting on a chair next to Terry's desk.

"I can see getting involved with this cat. She's such an exceptional feline, so lovable."

"Can you imagine," I said, "we've owned our property for over twenty years, but it wasn't until last week when Precious and I walked down to the brook that I knew we had a blackberry patch. We spent hours just picking berries and listening to the brook gurgle. Where have I been? What have I been doing?"

"You've been so busy trying to survive, you haven't taken time to stop and smell the roses. It's time you and Muriel slow down and start enjoying yourselves."

Good advice from such a young woman. The studio made a perfect office. Bookshelves lined the end walls. The other two sides of the room were all glass windows allowing the magnificent view to face me when I sat at my desk. The late summer sun mellowed the walnut panelled walls. On cool fall mornings I started a fire in the brick fireplace.

Terry stood looking at the view. "This is really beautiful," she commented. "I wish I could be married someplace like this.

"Let's do it." I answered.

"What?"

"You. Have your wedding here on the mountain."

"I-I couldn't do that. You know I'm having a small wedding. Just the two families, you and Muriel. I couldn't afford a wedding this setting deserves.

"Nonsense. You're having two attendants and a reception in the church hall. Just switch it up here." I didn't see a problem. "Muriel and I will give you your reception as a wedding present. Lord knows I owe you much more than that."

"I couldn't let you do that. Besides, it's too far to travel."

"We'll charter a bus. Everyone can meet at the Latham Mall. Hop the bus—Presto—they're here. We'll have one big party. Come on. I know how tough it has been since your dad got sick and has been out of work. Hopefully, you will only get married once. You should have what you want. Please?" I pleaded.

Terry's head shook back and forth, but in her heart I sensed that she really wanted to be married on our mountain. I wore her down.

"OK, OK. On one condition. You let Precious be in the wedding party."

"Precious?" I whooped.

"Yes. You know how much I love this cat. I'm going to miss this little rascal." Precious loved Terry, too. She was helping the bride-to-be take supplies from boxes.

It's your wedding," I said." I can't guarantee how she'll behave. You can expect most anything."

The weather was perfect for this special occasion. The wedding party arrived on Saturday. It felt good to have a crowd around us. This is what our house was originally intended to support—lots of people having loads of fun.

Six older cats scattered, not to be seen again until Sunday night. Precious hadn't forgotten her manners. She greeted each guest when he or she came through the door. She looked much more presentable than on her debut Thanksgiving Day the year before. All her fur had grown in, and she was shampooed, brushed and groomed to perfection.

She kept guests occupied while caterers went about their work of setting up, decorating and cooking.

I checked with Terry once more to make sure she wanted Precious as the ring bearer. The bride was confident about her little furry friend. Muriel played the organ while all the guests took their seats in the great outdoors. A white lattice rose arbor separated the spacious lawns. The roses had long since lost their blooms, but the trellis was alive with fall-colored mum blossoms. Grass, although tinged with tan, showed green. Guests faced the wide open space and view to the south. The colorful foliage, clear bright blue sky and distant mountain range gave the effect of a wide screen cinamescope. Blooming mum plants matched the colors of the wedding party gowns.

The sound of the wedding march filtered out of the house into the noonday air.

The first person to start out on the white linen runner was the groom's seven-year-old sister Lisa, scattering flower petals as she walked. Behind her, but coming at a much faster pace, was Precious. She caught up with the little girl, then darted around her.

Voices raised in concern. I jumped to my feet, ready to go after the cat. I had told Terry to expect anything. Once in front of the flower girl, however, the cat slowed down and stopped in front of the minister where Greg waited. She waited with them until Lisa arrived.

Precious jogged back up the runner to greet the

attendants, escorted each one to the altar. Each time the cat ran back up the runner, the white satin saddle bags fastened around her middle to hold the rings jounced from side to side. I envisioned the rings flying off the miniature satin pillows and everyone on their hands and knees looking for the small gold bands. Her miniature rosebud-covered collar lost a few buds, but the rings remained intact inside their satin envelope.

Several minutes of applause and chants rang through the hills as the cat escorted Terry to her place beside Greg. "Way to go Precious! Way to go!"

The cat looked up the runner, saw no one else to escort down the aisle. She didn't know what to do. I held her until time to present the rings. Precious walked over to Greg, bushy tail held high. She stood perfectly still, like a horse waiting to be mounted, while Greg removed the ring from the saddle bag pillow. Big yellow eyes stayed fixed on Greg's hand as he slipped the gold band on Terry's finger.

Terry reached down to retrieve the other ring. Precious saw her crying. "Iow, iow. Eeo, eeo," she said.

"Yes, love, I'm all right. I love you, too," Terry whispered and gave the cat a pat on the head. Precious moved closer to her young friend. I started towards the cat, but Terry signaled it was all right, to let her be.

The words, "I now pronounce you husband and wife. You may kiss the bride," sounded in the stillness of the day. The newlyweds embraced, the silhouette of a black cat between them. Shouts of congratulations filled the air. Organ music again filtered through the open window.

At the beginning of the ceremony the bride walked to the altar on the arm of her father, carrying a bouquet of white and pale pink roses. She left on the arm of her new husband, carrying a fluffy black and white cat.

Terry and Greg made a handsome looking couple.

Her strawberry blonde hair fell gracefully on her slender shoulders. Greg's deep brown eyes glowed. His dark curly hair blew gently in the fall breeze.

Before getting into the limousine that would take the couple to Albany Airport and a trip to Disney World, Terry hugged and kissed the cat. "You are such a darling. And so good. You made my day, honey, and you are simply Precious."

"Iow, iow."

"I love you too, Sweetie. See you in two weeks."

Muriel, Precious and I stood by the bus door. Each passenger expressed appreciation and thanked Precious for being such a wonderful hostess.

One lady remarked, "I've never seen anything like this cat. I've had cats all my life but none were like this one. You certainly gave her the right name."

An uproar came from inside the bus. "Three cheers for Precious. Hip-hip-hooray."

I asked myself why it was every time we got involved with anything or anyone, Muriel and I always ended up taking a back seat to this fur ball. And we call them dumb animals!

Muriel made arrangements to stay with a friend in Schenectady for the winter. She came home weekends. That gave me one less concern to think about—her getting stuck in a two-foot snow drift on the way home. I acquired a new office worker, Precious.

Precious didn't have a very steady hand. Blue, green, and orange marker lines zig-zagged across my charts. Paperwork flew as she scratched. Clients were disappointed when I didn't bring her with me. They all adored her and spoiled her rotten. She enjoyed every minute of it. She was a people animal.

We had an exceptionally snowy winter. High piles of snow were still along the road in March. Precious was restless the latter part of Friday afternoon. She wasn't content just to be with me. She insisted on being on my lap, up around my chin. "EIOW, EIOW." She jumped off my lap, ran to the front door and back. "EIOW, EIOW." She grabbed my leg and let out with a piercing "RROW, RROW."

"What's wrong with you, cat?" I scolded. There was no one at the door. The other cats were sleeping.

Precious wouldn't let up. Back and forth to the front door while giving forth with mournful S.O.S. calls. It was between 6:30 and 7 p.m., and Muriel still wasn't home. I picked up the cat and tried to calm her down. I had no idea what she was trying to tell me or what was wrong with her. "Muriel will be home shortly. Everything's OK," I kept saying.

Precious jumped from my arms just as the telephone rang. Muriel was in the emergency room at Ellis Hospital in Schenectady. "I fell in the plant about 4:30 and broke my wrist," she said.

That's about the time Precious started acting up. "Please come and get me. I'm in terrible pain and can't drive."

Her voice was teary. There was no leaving my four-legged companion behind. We went to bring our friend home.

Precious wouldn't let Muriel out of her sight. She inspected the ugly arm cast before she curled up alongside of her friend on the bed.

Until now this cat had never gone into Muriel's bedroom—never. But she was there now. Every move Muriel made, little Florence Nightingale was on her four feet. She even followed Muriel to the bathroom and waited outside the door.

The break wasn't the usual broken wrist. The entire wrist area was shattered, requiring extensive surgery and therapy. A dinner bell was set on the night stand. If I didn't respond immediately to its ring, the cat would be on my case. From "Eiow, Eiow" to "EIOW, EIOW!"

The cat refused to leave the bedroom to eat or even go potty. I set up a snack tray along side of the bed with cat food on it and put the litter pan outside the bathroom door.

The routine was simple. When the patient ate, the nurse ate. When the patient went to the bathroom, so did the cat. When Muriel washed or slept, Precious did too. So much for finding good office help. I had to go it alone.

Therapy was painful and dragged out for months. At first, the exercises baffled the fur-covered assistant. She liked the weighted cord being rolled up around the broom handle. Big yellow eyes followed the weights as they moved sideways and up. Paws gave the string a swat, trying to catch it. However, climbing the wall with the hand was just plain boring.

Therapy advanced to squeezing balls and trying to grasp soup cans. Muriel and I sat at opposite ends of the long dining room table. I'd roll the ball, she'd try to grab it. Precious sat on the steps leading to the studio-office and watched the ball make its way from one end of the table to the other. By the time the ball had rolled to the edge, the cat had become impatient. She jumped up on the table, intercepted the ball like a soccer pro, and continued to push the soft white round thing towards her sick friend.

That was fun. Let's do it again. Once in awhile the ball veered off the table, but most of the time Precious had better aim than Muriel.

Our lives bustled with activity. Ice packs, therapy, x-rays, cast changes and exercises. (I still didn't have any office help. Terry came to the rescue.)

Spring brought with it the usual muddy, debris-strewn yard. I tried to stay inside until the ground dried out. Plus—

spring turkey season was here. Hunters traveled our road in search of the birds. Bullets whizzed by from all directions.

It was mid Saturday morning. Muriel and Precious finished their exercises and Muriel was reading. Precious curled up in her lap. I kidded her about spending time with the other six felines.

"They don't even come near me," she said. So much for quality time.

I adjusted slide bars, volume and tried new sounds on the organ. A sour note sometimes gave Precious cause to raise her head in disapproval and cast me a look that said, "Better try that one again." What did she want from me?

Muriel was the accomplished musician. I played the organ for my own enjoyment and relaxation.

I was a heavy smoker in my youth. My doctor and husband insisted I cut down. Dr. Kinard suggested I smoke a pipe if I must smoke. He said, "Oh, not out in public, but it isn't as deadly as cigarettes."

Irv thought the suggestion hilarious and bought me a corn cob pipe. Like Nero who fiddled while Rome burned, an old corn cob pipe burned while I played the organ that Saturday morning.

A knock came on the front door. A quick glance told me it was a stranger. Most men in our area had shaggy hair, beards or unshaven faces. They rarely wore new clothes. In the doorway stood a medium-built man with trimmed hair and clean face. His apparel looked as if he just came from L. L. Bean. His new boots were laden with mud.

The bright orange cap came off as he introduced himself. "I'm Winchester Canfield," he said. His name matched his general appearance. "Do you know where I might contact a tow service? My vehicle is mired down in the state land." He talked funny.

I introduced myself and motioned him into the front hall. "How mired down are you?" I asked, mimicking his pronunciation. "Maybe I can pull you out. I own a four-wheel drive International Scout with a winch and heavy tow ropes."

"I couldn't impose on your generosity," he answered in his polite, well-bred manner. He spotted the telephone.

"You have a telephone?"

"Sure. We've got lights and running water, too."

"I'm sorry" he apologized, "but you're so isolated from the nearest village I didn't think you'd be granted such services."

I tried to ease his embarrassment. "The Federal Government has a radar tower on top of our mountain to the left. I gave them permission to run their lines over our property. Feel free to use the phone."

He removed his muddy boots before tromping across the highly polished floor. That alone told me he was a stranger. People from our area would carry the mud with them.

I heard him say, "I'm all right. Someone's going to try to release my vehicle from the mud. . .Yes, I'll call before I depart for home."

He told me he used his credit card. He also said he didn't want to impose on my day or interrupt my activity. By now Muriel was in the hall, overcome by curiosity. She introduced herself and Precious. "Oh, you're not interrupting anything. Precious and I were reading the *Wall Street Journal*. This will be a nice diversion. Precious gets upset when she sees how the stock market is going."

Muriel expected to get a chuckle out of the young man, but he shot a quizzical look at Muriel—then me.

"Which one of you ladies is Muriel?" he asked, his finger moving back and forth. We went into the Muriel explanation.

"You're not interrupting anything," I told him.

"Just let me turn off the switch on the organ. I was playing when you knocked."

A strange look came over Winchester's face. "Y-you were playing the organ? Thank God. I thought I heard organ music while tromping down this desolate path. I felt it was an omen. I—I was sure I'd be lost in this wilderness forever."

I grabbed my gloves and corn cob pipe. Precious was right behind me. Winchester helped Muriel onto the back seat of the Scout. I pulled tow ropes from their brackets in the carriage house and threw them into the cargo area. Bean's catalogue model waited for me to get in, closed the door and went to the other side of the Scout.

When he opened the passenger's door, Precious jumped up on the front seat and sat next to me.

The fellow wearing the spotless buffalo plaid pants didn't get in. He was calm but emphatic. "Your cat is in the vehicle. I'll just put her down outside here."

Precious didn't wait for me to respond. She began her series of comments and reprimands but didn't budge from my side.

"I prefer not to ride with your cat," the visitor said, still outside.

"Then we better go back in the house so you can call a tow truck—excuse me, a tow service. This cat goes everywhere with me," I said.

I opened the Scout door and started to get out. Winchester slid onto the front seat next to Precious.

There was dead silence for the first few minutes. Muriel was bursting at the seams, trying not to explode into laughter. We moved past the last turnoff in the state land. There wasn't even a dirt path to follow, just a trace of where another vehicle had broken and pushed down the undergrowth. Saplings bent and snapped as the Scout bounced over them. The proper gentleman asked if we'd mind if he smoked.

"Not at all, if you don't object if I do."

I dug my corn cob from my pocket. Utter shock clouded his face. (I knew this would get him.)

He shook his head and muttered under his breath, "Why does this surprise me?"

Muriel declined a cigarette. She doesn't smoke. He struck a match to his. It must have been some foreign brand. It smelled like dirty socks. Precious put her paw over her face. We trounced further into the wilderness. "How did you get so far off the beaten path?" I asked.

"I was turkey hunting. Today is the last day of the spring season. I'll be disappointed should I be forced to go home empty handed." He looked at his expensive watch. "I could still capture a prize if you are able to free my vehicle quickly."

The prize of stupidity came to mind. I glanced at my Timex. It was 10:30 a.m. Turkey season ended at noon. No way would I let this greenhorn loose in the woods. He might kill himself.

The land descended into a meadow. Spring rains had turned the lowlands into a swamp. "Mired down" didn't adequately describe the predicament. The Lincoln was buried to the hub caps. It had to be pulled out backwards.

Winchester tried to figure out how we could attach the tow ropes and winch to the rear frame without getting soaked with mud. Any idiot could see there was no easy solution. I pulled on my rubber boots, wound tow rope around my shoulder, grabbed the end of the winch and headed for the pool of stagnant sludge. Precious was right on my heels. She had to back off when the muddy water reached her middle. The Lincoln's owner stood on the edge of the muddy mess offering suggestions.

Simply Precious   49

Precious returned to solid dry ground. Muriel could see the look on the cat's face. Before she could reach the cat, this feline was prancing back and forth in front of the new boots. "EIOW. EIOW. ERRO. ERRO. $#!@*" (You don't want to know what that last one means.)

Black flies were out in swarms. The mud puddle served as the perfect breeding ground. Winchester swatted at his face. I tried to keep my mouth closed for more reasons than one. Muriel also swatted while Precious shook her head back and forth.

Winchester remarked, "My God! What are these things? Even the cat's having problems with them." He might have thought the flies were getting to this feline, but he was the true center of her distraction. She probably wondered what stupid fool could get himself into such a situation. It wasn't easy tugging at this heavy object. The Lincoln outweighed the Scout by many pounds. Engines raced, and gobs of mud splattered the Scout's windshield.

Finally, all four wheels of the Lincoln were on dry ground. Both vehicles, Precious and I wore enough mud to mud wrestle. Winchester no longer had crisp new-looking clothes, either.

We were about five hundred feet from home when Muriel saw a turkey gobbler strut near the road's edge. I slammed on the brakes. Both Precious and Muriel got out. "Chase him back into the wood, girl!" Muriel yelled to the cat. "That's it! It's fifteen minutes till noon. I don't want this bird to land in a pot."

Winchester stood on the roadside, gun drawn. I yelled, "What do you think you're doing? Put that thing away."

"I'm going after that turkey. Why did she and that cat chase it?"

I pushed the gun towards the ground. "Not on our property you won't. Our land is posted. You can't hunt here. Haven't you had enough grief for one day?" I asked. "Besides, the turkey's confused. His clock must be fast. He thought it was noon time. Most wildlife can sense when it's safe and when it isn't." The hunter reluctantly put the gun into the car.

"Unload it," I ordered. He removed the shells from the chamber.

Back at the house Winchester made another telephone call. "Yes, I'm fine. Yes... I should he home in two hours. I'll tell you when I arrive. You're not going to believe it anyway."

Winchester Canfield thanked me for my assistance. We removed most of the mud from his clothes. He offered to pay me, but I declined. (This experience was priceless to me.) We stood on the front porch. His eyes scanned the surrounding mountains.

"You have beautiful country up here, but I doubt if I'll ever return."

I thought, "Thank God for small favors."

He looked lost. "I don't know how I'm going to explain this day to my wife and friends."

"What do you mean?" I questioned." You got stuck. We pulled you out. Simple as that."

"Oh, no." It was the first time I had seen him smile. "How I got stuck to begin with—hearing organ music in the middle of nowhere—stumbling on you two— two women with the same uncommon first name—one who smokes a corncob pipe—both think turkeys can tell time and their cat reads the *Wall Street Journal* and follows the stock market—no one's going to believe me." He sounded almost condescending as he added, "You two have been in the wilderness too long."

He looked down at the cat washing mud from her paws and fur. "You have one of the most contemptible cats I have ever seen. I detest cats." Precious stopped washing, strutted back and forth in front of muddy boots. "@/%#," she said.

"I don't think she likes you very much either." I chuckled. "Have a safe trip home and please—stay off back ròads."

Tuesday after our towing escapade, Muriel had a doctor's appointment. Precious was all over her, wouldn't leave Muriel alone. The cat and I remained in the car while a new cast was put on her wrist. I rarely spoke harshly to Precious but there was no calming her down. On the ride home the cat climbed all over my injured friend. We didn't know what she was trying to tell us.

The telephone was ringing when we opened the front door. It was Muriel's sister in New Jersey. Their father had been found dead in bed that morning. So that was what Precious was trying to tell Muriel. The cat's keen perception and instincts frightened us. How did she know?

Cat-sitting arrangements were made for our two-day absence. Upon our return, Precious appeared to be sick. She was quiet, listless and wouldn't eat. The veterinarian said it was melancholy. The cat grieved the same as Muriel.

"Come on," I said. "You mean to tell me this cat can detect and experience grief?"

"This isn't uncommon," the doctor said. "Many pets express awareness of trouble and grief. Newspapers are filled with such encounters. Then too, you left her alone. She might have felt a sense of abandonment. You've never left her alone overnight since you've had her. Not all animals have this extra sense, but those who do sometimes become possessive towards humans." Dr. Aaronson scratched Precious's ears, hugged and kissed her. "I told you this cat is special. If she doesn't snap out of it by next week, bring her back."

Within the week Precious was back to her old self. We never left her alone overnight again. If the cat couldn't go, neither would we, no matter what the circumstances. We also scrutinized any of Precious's strange behavior with much apprehension and concern, asking ourselves, "What's happening that we don't know about but will, shortly?"

Muriel's injury caused a twenty-five percent loss of the use of her right hand. She was forced to retire from grass cutting for that summer. We hired someone to cut the grass. As much as Precious had loved riding the mower, she ignored the machine now. She didn't trust a stranger at the helm of the ship she had navigated. The cat was content to stay with her friend. This feline enjoyed being a mother hen. She was even condescending towards the other fur-covered residents. She continued to ride with me whenever possible. Every time the car went out the driveway, Precious felt she should be in it.

Muriel's new car was due for service in late June. While the car was on the lift, Precious was underneath it, making sure the mechanic hit all the grease fittings.

Cheri Flannery, the garage owner and friend, rushed out the door. "I can't stay and chat," she said. "The factory rep is here together with dealers from five other agencies. The manufacturer is converting all our manual accounting systems to computerized on-line status. It's a mess. How about sitting in on the meeting? You might be able to offer some insight to what's happening. Lord knows—the rest of us are baffled."

"What will I do with Precious? I can't leave her in the car. Can she stay in your office?" I asked.

"That's where the meeting is, but she won't be any trouble. She never is. In fact, she'll be company for my dogs. I'm picking them up from the groomers, stopping for Danish and will be right back. Tell Harrison Grant to start the meeting without me." She was gone.

Grant introduced me to everyone and placed another chair next to Cheri's within the circle of dealers already seated. He whispered, "Don't be surprised at anything that might transpire. We're having a devil of a time with this conversion. Cheri told me about you. Feel free to jump in at any time." He turned to take his seat. "Nice cat," he remarked and gave Precious a scratch under her chin.

Tension could be cut with a knife as Jim Donovan, the factory rep, opened the meeting. Fifteen minutes into the meeting, Cheri returned. Her two prize-winning circus-performing dogs bounded in behind her. The meeting stopped, dead in its tracks, while the two celebrities, Beauty—a lop-eared Basset Hound, and Tar Baby, a black Labrador—greeted their friends, including Precious, then went to the stranger.

The speaker was in shock as he reluctantly acknowledged the handshake from Tar Baby, but he ignored Beauty's stubby paw. The paw went out again and once more it was ignored. Beauty grabbed the man's pant leg and gently tugged.

"He won't leave until you shake hands with him," explained the dog's owner.

In complete disgust, the man from Michigan bent down and took the paw. The dogs settled down at Cheri's feet. She motioned for Precious to join them.

"Now will you please remove the animals so we can continue?" Donovan pled.

Harrison Grant, from Dorset, was on his feet. "They

stay. These dogs are an important part of our communities. The cat is their friend. She stays, too." He smiled at the fur-covered guests and continued, "Let's get on with this."

A deafening discussion followed. The dogs interpreted some of the words as commands directed to them and went into their act of jumps, roll-overs and barks. Precious jumped at the chance to show her drill sergeant's authority. She chased after the canines with her own version of the day's commands. I started after the cat but Cheri's arm went out in front of me. She shook her head. A moment later Cheri's voice could be heard above the commotion. The dogs came back to her and sat. Precious followed suit.

A roar of laughter shattered the argument but infuriated Jim Donovan. Completely unnerved and shaking his head furiously, he said, "I don't believe this. Don't you people take anything seriously? I must insist this zoo be kept under control or I'll remove these animals myself. They have no business being here in the first place."

Grant ignored the wisecrack about the animals and picked up the conversation where it had ended before the circus act began.

"OK. Simmer down," Donovan told him." We aren't reenacting the Boston Tea Party."

"Oh, yes, we are," came the snappy reply. "Michigan is trying to tell us what we can and cannot do. As long as it doesn't jeopardize the manufacturer's required financial reports, they have no say as to how we should run our operations. This isn't Detroit or Dallas. This is rural New England. Human factors are more important to us then cut-and-dried money transactions."

He glanced at the dogs and cat watching and listening to his every word. "Why these dogs here have raised more money for local charities than we make from selling your damn cars. So let's move on to things we do agree on."

Tempers raged, words flew, voices blared. The animals went into another act. Again I was signaled not to curtail Precious. After several minutes, Cheri summoned the animals to her side. The young man from Michigan conceded. Calmness fell over the meeting.

All prepared data was ready for transmittal to Michigan.

"You'll be surprised to see how easy this is," Donovan remarked." These red lights will blink when the line begins to transmit."

He dialed the special telephone number. Nothing happened. He dialed again. Still nothing. The dealers didn't try to conceal their sneers. Both Tar Baby and Precious watched the computer screen without moving a muscle. Beauty was sprawled out in the middle of the floor snoring.

Donavan jerked the phone from its cradle and dialed once more. He grinned with satisfaction when the machine beeped, red lights bounced back and forth. Suddenly, everything stopped. Smoke poured from and around the machine. BANG! The front cover blew off the computer.

The explosion clued the dogs for another performance. Precious followed in her usual manner. In the middle of all this commotion the town's fire whistle wailed. A garage mechanic, who was also a volunteer fireman, poked his head in the door, yelling, "Hathaway's General Store is on fire. All the fireworks for the Fourth are in there!"

In a flash he was gone taking the five male dealers with him. Firecrackers skyrocketed in the distance. The manufacturer's rep was left with Cheri, the two dogs, Precious and me. Cheri calmed the dogs. I picked up the cat. Donovan tried to figure out what happened.

Smoke continued to spew from the wall in back of the computer. Precious jumped from my arms and started to howl. "RROW, RROW." I knew what that sound meant, so I hurried to her side. Donavan and Cheri jumped.

"What's wrong? Is she all right?" Cheri asked.

The wall outlet was smoldering. I grabbed the fire extinguisher from the far wall and sprayed. I pointed to the charred wall.

"Here's your problem," I said. "Computers require their own line. You have other things plugged into that outlet. There must have been a power dip or surge when the fire broke out at Hathaways. The wall was on fire. That's why Precious howled. She has a special sense for trouble."

Cheri understood the cat's special gift, but Donavan gave a skeptical stare.

"What do we do now?" Cheri asked.

Donavan held the distorted disk in his hand. "You can bet I'm not going through another day like today. You Yankees are crazy." He turned to me. "Would you be interested in this project? I'll authorize payment. It might be better if a native worked with this conversion. Since you seemed unshaken by today's antics, working with this group should be a breeze. I'm used to more conventional types of business operations."

Cheri nodded her approval. I had another client—a national automobile manufacturer. Jim Donavan smiled for the first time since he had arrived. "What the hell—let's go watch the fireworks." He tossed the warped disk towards the waste basket.

Tar Baby caught it and brought it back. Cheri bent down, whispered something to the dogs and told Precious to join the dogs in the doorway. Donavan gave her a scathing look. "You set me up with these animals, didn't you?"

Cheri sported a smirk and shrugged her shoulders.

"Yes, you did," he said, shaking his finger at her, "but maybe I deserved it."

The dogs sat in the doorway waiting to shake hands. Jim got down on his haunches, shook hands with Tar Baby and Beauty. Precious waited. He picked the cat up and gave her a hug.

"You're a smart kitty," he told the cat. She returned his affection with a forceful nudge with her head that sent him off balance and to the floor. The dogs gave his face a bath. Donavan wiped his wet chin with his sleeve. "Thanks guys. I need some friends right about now."

Precious was in her glory for the nine weeks I worked at the car dealership. She romped with her two canine friends while I completed the computer conversion. She didn't once seem to miss not taking our walks along our dirt road.*

Hunters, Precious and I weren't the only ones who traveled our dirt road. Local riding club members pushed by on horseback, and bicycle enthusiasts strengthened their leg muscles on our steep hills, picking up speed on the flat section in front of our house. One day a faded blue pickup truck went by our house very slowly. About the same place where Muriel had chased the turkey, it stopped. A door opened and closed. Several minutes later the truck went back down the road, picking up speed as it passed our house.

*AUTHOR'S NOTE. Jim Donavan eventually bought Flannery's dealership. Beauty passed away. Cheri retired Tar Baby from performing. The dog enjoyed being at the garage so much, Cheri gave Tar Baby to Donavan. The dog was stretched out on his cedar mat next to Jim Donavan's desk when Precious and I went to the garage to have our car serviced. I guess we Yankees weren't as crazy as the man from Michigan thought.

Simply Precious

Precious began to prance, jump up my leg and howled "RROW, RROW!"

That cry brought Muriel and me to our feet. When Muriel opened the front door Precious ran through her legs and started up the driveway—screeching all the way.

Muriel called to the cat but it was useless. Precious was already running up the road, pantaloons and tail flying in the breeze. As we reached the road's edge the cat ran back to us. Relieved, we waited.

"RROW, RROW!" Then back up the road she jogged.

She stopped at the spot where the pickup truck had been seen just moments earlier. We surveyed the area but found nothing unusual. Precious went over the wall, wailing as she went. Muriel climbed to the top of the three feet of piled stone and looked down into the wood fern and goldenrod.

Next to the cat lay a motionless shape. "RROW, RROW!" I cautioned Muriel to be careful. We didn't know what kind of animal it was or if the creature was alive or dead. It was a small shaggy gray and white dog with black eyes. It was still alive, but barely. Muriel held Precious while I inspected the animal's condition.

The stranger in the pickup must have hit the dog and brought it up on our road to dispose of it. We took an old blanket from the back seat of the Scout, placed the injured dog in it and carried him to the tail gate. Before the tail gate closed, the cat jumped in and jabbered in cat language to the injured fur-covered stranger.

There was no prying Precious loose from her vigil. All the way to the vet's the cat was beside the dog, trying to comfort him. Before Dr. Aaronson could complete his examination, the animal died. I paid the bill. The doctor said he would bury the dog in his cemetery. He was not wearing a collar or license.

Simply Precious

Precious was very quiet all the way home. She snuggled into Muriel's arms while we praised her for her efforts.

"Sorry it didn't work out, pal," Muriel told the cat. "But because of you, he wasn't left to die alone." My blood boiled. How could anyone be so cruel? It made me sick to think of it. We searched for the pickup to no avail. Most trucks that traveled our road were beat up with faded blue or red paint. From that day on, we closely examined every strange vehicle that came up our road as it went by.

Late that fall we again witnessed Precious's uncanny ability to detect trouble. Little Eva succumbed to old age. Although Precious had not been close to the animal, she was the one who led us upstairs to the body. The other felines expressed no sense of loss.

Muriel once again stayed in the city and came home on weekends. The nation's economy was on a slide. Interest rates soared to two digits. Many companies that had planned on computerizing their accounting systems backed down. I had a lot of free time on my hands. I kept busy doing chores around the house, straightening up the carriage house and equipment shed. Precious was discontented. She wanted some action and wanted to enjoy it with me.

While rummaging through the equipment shed I came across my skis. I hadn't been on those long skinny boards in years. I had skied downhill on the slopes of Lake Placid many years ago. Now I had miles of wide open spaces in my own back yard to explore cross country.

The first few outings I soon found out I wasn't on the slopes now and was a few years older. Precious made such fuss when I left her home that I'd put her in my back pack and away we'd go. When she got chilled, she snuggled down inside the pack on her red jacket.

Sometimes I'd pack a lunch and we'd eat by the brook or set a table on a large rock ledge overlooking the glen. The snow was clean and undisturbed but for the ski trail.

Once in a while we went out at night when the moon was full. A more beautiful sight I've never seen. I poled to the crunch and swish of my runners gliding over the blanket of white. The stillness was emphasized by the long motionless shadows stretching across the fields. The snow caught the moon's rays peeking over the mountain and sparkled like diamonds. Everything appeared to be caught up in the vacuum of motionless splendor. These special moments were ours—my fur-covered friend's and mine.

On dark clear nights Precious and I looked out through the studio window, up into the sky blanketed with millions of stars. Two big yellow eyes, two big brown eyes, staring into space. The celestial spectacular seemed so close I felt I could reach up and scoop a handful of bright shining dots. The silence was deafening. God's presence was everywhere.

I had always been too busy to notice such things. It took a restless cat to make me appreciate the beauty that surrounded me every day.

Contented or not, we managed to survive the winter without mishaps. Little Phella was ailing. He died in the spring. Our pet cemetery was getting larger under the butternut tree at the north end of our lawn.

My business telephone was silent much of the time. At last in March I was commissioned to convert a large national distributor's accounting system. Precious was in her glory. Trips to the city—Terry coming to the office to help when needed.

On a beautiful spring day I started out the stepping stone walk to my car. I noticed that the name sign on the lamp post was dangling. A wind storm the previous night had snapped the link in one of the chains.

I took a pair of pliers and tightened the links. I stepped back to see if I had evened them. I missed my footing and slipped off the wooden planter area. The next thing I knew, I was up against the kitchen wall on my knees, my left leg bent around under my right one. It took several minutes before I could get back up on my feet, but I seemed to be all right.

I could hear Precious's cries inside the house. I went back in the house to assure my friend I was OK. "Eeo, eeo," she chirped.

"Yes, Sweetie. I'm all right. See you tonight."

By the time I arrived home that night, I couldn't walk. My left knee was swollen to twice its normal size. Precious volunteered her nursing skills and stayed with me. The next morning Muriel called the Rescue Squad. Precious helped me dress, but I couldn't get my shoes on. My foot was too swollen. As Muriel handed me my shirt I remarked, "I hope you told them to send a strong crew. I'm no lightweight."

"Oh, stop your fussing. Ambulance Corps members are trained for this work."

Oh yeah? What followed after the emergency squad arrived would put the Keystone Cops to shame. Three people stormed the house, looking as if they were practicing for the Cripples Anonymous Marathon. There was a young girl, about twenty, weighing in at about three hundred pounds. I felt I should try to help her up the front steps, she had so much trouble walking. Pain was written all over her face.

Behind her, a little old lady who looked ninety and may have tipped the scales at ninety pounds struggled up the steps. Bringing up the rear was a little old man of about the same physical description. The three of them together didn't look as if they could pick up a bushel basket let alone my two hundred pounds of dead weight.

I was correct in my assumption. I managed to get on the gurney with Muriel's help. I felt I was trying to catch a bobsled. The apparatus was in constant motion. The "trained" crew proceeded to drop me down the five *steps head first!* Precious let out a yell. Somebody stepped on her. Muriel grabbed the cat while the three stooges tried to maneuver their patient over the stepping stone walk to the Emergency Truck. I made the suggestion to back the vehicle to the front porch, but I was overruled.

Once in the driveway, no one could figure out how to lift me up into the vehicle. The gurney was raised to the maximum height. As a last resort, I slid my rear end around, put my right foot on the bumper of the vehicle, grabbed the side of the door opening with both hands and belly flopped inside. I then rolled over onto the flattened stretcher. The legs of the gurney were raised. My legs burned with pain.

Just as "grandpa" was about to close the back doors of the truck, Precious wriggled from Muriel's grip, jumped down, and made a giant leap inside the vehicle. She pounced up onto my stomach. "Eeo, eeo"— then hissed at the attending paramedic. The young girl was scared silly. She thought the cat was going to attack her.

Muriel ran after the cat, calling, "Precious! No! You can't go."

The cat just looked at Muriel with a smug expression. "That's what you think. I'm stayin'." She sat on my middle and washed herself. Muriel jumped into her car and followed the red flashing light and wailing sirens. The sound penetrated the hills. It certainly cleared our dirt road of any traffic—squirrels, rabbits, deer or turkeys.

In the excitement of the added passenger, the paramedic neglected to secure the gurney. With every turn and hill in the road, I was either going backwards, forward or sideways. Once Precious tried to come up near my face to tell me if we go down, we go together—but we took a sharp curve and she went sailing onto the floor. She shook herself off and hopped right back on top of me. The paramedic was too scared to argue with her. The gurney was still loose as a goose.

I yelled, "Slow this thing down before we all get killed. What's the big hurry?" We had already come down the worst of it. The road flattened out. The rush continued as they lowered me to the ground at the hospital. My head was lower than my feet. In their efforts to level me, the gurney almost upset. Again, Precious went flying off my stomach. And, once more she jumped back up.

Someone hollered, "What the devil was that? Get that cat out of here!"

The back seat paramedic replied, "Unless you want your eyes scratched out, you'd better leave it alone."

Precious sat on my chest. Her lips curled up, showing teeth. Muriel came to the rescue, removed my bodyguard and went inside.

Two hospital attendants began to run with me as if I were bleeding to death. My past and future whirled in front of me. I already knew my past—and what my future was likely to be if they didn't slow down with that damned go-kart. Strange—this wasn't the way it happened on TV's "Trapper John."

The doctor remarked, "There are no broken bones,

but you may wish there were before you are finished with this."

All the tendons were damaged in my knee. It would be a long and painful recovery.

The emergency room nurse measured me for crutches. The two sticks given me were different lengths. Muriel and the cat looked on as another pair of crutches came on the scene. The nurse swung the pieces of wood towards me. Precious thought I was being attacked. She made a flying leap and caught the woman in the thigh. Muriel tried to apologize as she released the claws. The woman in white was livid.

"You're facing a lawsuit. Get that thing out of here, immediately. What's it doing in here, anyway? Animals aren't allowed in here."

The girl behind the desk tried to camouflage her amusement. "I wouldn't make too much of this if I were you. If anyone has the right to sue it's Mrs. Hine. Wait until you hear what our emergency squad did to her. The cat was only trying to protect its master. She's been perfectly calm until you wheeled that crutch. And we have no signs saying NO PETS ALLOWED."

"Excuse me," I interrupted. "These crutches aren't mates either. One is heavier than the other."

The nurse with the attitude jerked the crutches from under my arms, sending me into a tail spin. Muriel had control of the cat.

"They're the same *height!*" she bellowed, slamming the wooden sticks back into my hands and disappearing into the adjoining room.

"Wow! What an attitude!" I remarked. The receptionist apologized through fits of laughter. "Don't pay any attention to Denton. She hates herself most of the time. Patients have complained about her attitude for years. The personnel director has tried to get rid of her, but she is a good nurse. Just overworked. She'll be brought on the carpet for your situation. That was completely un-called for. We can't seem to get good ambulance volun-teers." She went over to the cat. "You're simply precious," she said. "And to think it took *you* to put that witch in her place. We've been trying to do that for years. Wait until the rest of the crew hears about this."

She was still laughing when she went back to her desk and picked up the telephone. "I'll have the rescue squad take you back home."

"No you won't," I said. "One ride with them is suffi-cient. I have a ride, thanks." I put the crutches, dubbed Frick and Frack, under my armpits and started out the door, barefoot. Muriel and Precious walked along side of me.

The following week I returned to the hospital to re-trieve my x-rays to take to my doctor in Albany. I noticed a big sign posted on the Emergency Room door: NO PETS ALLOWED. I wonder what enticed the hospital staff to do that?

Recovery was long and painful. Once again Florence Nightingale was at my side. Therapy was of a completely different nature from the routine for Muriel's injured wrist. There were no strings to paw, no balls to roll. Swinging my foot with a clamp-on weighted roller skate was what my doctor ordered, together with knee bending exercises.

Terry volunteered to help with my latest accounting conversion job. She and Precious worked at the long din-ing room table while I did my exercises. Muriel was my taxi on days I went to my client's office. Frick and Frack were returned to the hospital. I bought a pair of crutches that were mates.

Fourteen weeks later I was ordered to walk on my own and buy a treadmill exercise machine for days when I couldn't go outside. Every clear day, Precious and I walked up and down the flat section of road in front of our house. One hundred feet the first day. One hundred fifty feet the next—until I was able to walk a quarter of a mile without too much difficulty.

Precious would sometimes scamper ahead of me, chasing a leaf as the wind picked it up and carried it just beyond her reach. Chipmunks darted in and out of the stonewall fences, teasing the cat and daring her to chase them.

One day Precious had gone quite a distance ahead of me up the road. She stopped short, stretched her neck as she looked down into the berry patch to the west, then high-tailed it back to me as fast as she could. She seemed excited, yet her actions had a tinge of fright. I heard an unfamiliar sound. Precious jumped up my leg. She was shaking. She wanted to be picked up. I tried to soothe her but her body still trembled. Then I saw what had frightened her.

Mamma and two baby black cub bears were having a great time in our raspberry patch. I whispered to Precious to be very quiet. We didn't want to frighten them.

The mother bear must have weighed a good four hundred pounds and stood about seven feet tall as she raised up on her hind legs, extended her front paw and pulled the ripe berries within reach. Her cubs were feasting on fruit from shorter bushes. The baby bears were about the size of a large sheep dog. Their behinds were so round they toppled over when they stood up to pick the berries from higher bushes. Their mother was teaching them how to gather food. The cubs cleaned one section of bushes and romped around the field while mamma searched for more delicacies.

We stood on the road's edge until I could no longer stand on my feet. I carried Precious back to the house. She didn't want to get down. It was the only time I knew this cat to be afraid. The jet black coats of the bears were magnificent, and the gentleness with which the mother bear handled her young was amazing.

Had Precious not spied them first, I might have surprised the frolicking family. With that four-hundred-pound bear chasing me, both the cat and I would have met with disaster. I could barely walk. By no means could I run.

In a few weeks the berries were gone, and so were the bears. My walking companion and I made our way to the Beaver Pond at the end of our road entering state land. At first, the beavers slapped their tails, warning the others that there were strangers close by. After several visits they didn't seem to mind that Precious and I sat on the bank of the flooded pond and watched while the busy builders cut down trees, pushed them into place and rapped their flat tails in the mud.

Often we brought our lunch. When we did, we always left apples and bread for our busy little friends. Precious was spellbound when she saw those big fur-covered workers swim to and fro. Her eyes were glued to the saplings as they fell, and the long branched poles drifted to their final resting place in the Beaver Lodge. The cat was as intrigued as I. It was an educational experience for us both. In spite of my painful injury, I had a ball enjoying the great outdoors with my best friend.

Precious had trouble adapting to the treadmill. She didn't know how to walk on that contraption. When she got tired, instead of getting off, she flopped down on the belt which quickly carried her to the back and off the machine. She sat on the sidelines, studied the mechanism, jumped on, walked with me for about half a mile, jumped off and waited for me to complete my walk.

On painful, sleepless nights, I sat in the studio with Precious, our eyes searching the sky and fields, remembering the previous winter and the fun we'd had skiing in those wide open spaces of complete silence and beauty.

The first sign of daybreak is the alarm clock for creatures of the wild. Deer, turkeys and smaller animals of the woods roamed free and unafraid around our house. I've often been accused of not having enough apples for a pie, but my wild animals were always cared for with bales of hay, carrots, apples and corn.

Precious heard the sound first. She stretched her neck, put her face against the window and looked down. Three deer were in the flower bed below, chomping on a snowball bush. The shrub needed pruning, and the white tail deer did a fantastic job. Not one twig was left to be cleaned up. Unfortunately, they also sheared our Japanese yews. The tidbits may be a delicacy for the deer, but those shrubs are *off limits*. Wire now surrounds the healthy specimens to protect the branches from the landscape crew.

On the south lawn a group of five turkeys enjoyed their morning meal. These birds were at the feeder at exactly the same time each morning. (And Winchester Canfield questioned the turkey's ability to tell time? That shows how much he knew.)

Many a sunrise caught Precious and me eating a bowl of Rice Krispies while watching our outdoor friends enjoy their breakfast. The first time we snacked during the early dawn hours, I prepared only one bowl of cereal with fruit. My friend expressed her unwillingness to share the same bowl.

I placed two bowls on the small drop-leaf table against the window wall. Further complaints came from my dining companion. She had no fruit or sugar. Strawberries were too tart for her taste, but raspberries and bananas disappeared in short order. The only tip she gave me was to suggest I give her more milk the next time.

Our morning snacks became so frequent that the table remained set with place mats, sugar bowl, two cereal dishes and a box of Rice Krispies. I was allowed to leave the bouquet of wild flowers in the center of the table. Early dawn became a very special time for my friend and me. Watching our outdoor friends go about their day

and the cat's attentiveness to my aches and pains made
these hours more bearable.

After our accidents, Muriel and I went through dras-
tic changes for us on our mountain. Muriel didn't have
full use of her hand. My legs were shot. We made a great
pair. Precious was bored. The only outside activity she
enjoyed was visiting with employees of my clients. All but
one of our older pets had passed away. They were buried
beside the others near the butternut tree.

Clients spoiled Precious rotten. "I bought you this
toy, Precious."

"How about some catnip, Precious?"

"You sit here at the conference table, Precious."

Times when I didn't bring her, I heard, "Where's Precious?"

One trip I wished I hadn't brought my four-legged
friend along. I had to go into Albany one Saturday morning in early December to drop off paperwork to Terry,
who would work with employees to set the program in
motion for Monday morning.

Precious was restless. Against my better judgment, I
promised her she could go with me. I wrapped her in the
old red jacket, carried her to the Scout and put her on a
box in the front seat. The seats in the Scout didn't allow
the cat to look out through the window. I'd had the box
built for my road companion shortly after our encounter
with the mired Lincoln.

Precious made her rounds to the employees at my
client's office but seemed anxious to leave. She didn't
even want to spend time with Terry. She just wanted *out*.

Terry noticed the cat's unrest. "Is everything all right
up home? Precious never acts this way unless something's
happened."

"She's been like this all day. Maybe she's coming down with a cold or something. We'd better get going. Call me if you run into any problems with this program," I said and quickly made my exit.

Precious wouldn't sit still. She kept pacing back and forth across her box. I knew what these actions meant. Something must be wrong up home. I pushed the gas pedal down to a speed I rarely traveled.

Four miles from home, in Buskirk, we ran into a snow storm. Wind whirled at gust proportions. Snow came down so fast and heavy the windshield wipers couldn't push it off. I slowed down. Precious sat glued to her box, looking out through the swish of the wipers. Once she let out a chirp— "Eeo, eeo"

"Yes, honey. I'm fine. We'll soon be there. Hang on."

By the time we reached our road about four inches of snow had fallen. The storm was not only a surprise, it had the velocity of a blizzard. Wind slammed against the Scout, pulling the steering wheel from my grip. Thank God I was only five minutes from home.

I had no trouble churning up the mountain in my four-wheel drive Scout. We reached the top of the first hill which leveled off for about five hundred feet before the last incline faced us. The wheels churned. I zig-zagged with the wind, causing Precious to lose her balance and tumble to the floor. She hopped back up on her box only to find herself on the floor again, this time from me slamming on the brakes. An ash tree had come down across the road, blocking our way.

The tree was too big for me to struggle with. Stone wall fences lined both sides of the road so I couldn't go around through the field. I'd have to leave the Scout and walk the rest of the way. Lights from my living room window, a thousand feet ahead, served as a beacon in this blizzard.

The road ahead was a steep hill. I wasn't sure I could

---

make it—me with a bad leg, using a cane, carrying my purse, attache case and Precious. She couldn't walk through this snow. It was already halfway up her body.

I got back into the Scout and closed the door. Precious was on her box, making concerned noises. I gave her a hug, scratched her ears. "Eeo. Iow."

"Yes, I'm all right. I love you, too. We're both going to be OK, but you're going to have to cooperate with me. OK?"

She brushed her head against my face with an approving nudge. My attache case was not the usual hard covered, flat, rectangular style. It was semisoft, broad and deep, large enough to accommodate stacks of large computer printout sheets. I rearranged the papers on each side. I had left most of the contents of the case with Terry, leaving the center compartment empty. I put the red jacket in the open space, squeezed the cat into the opening and covered her head with part of the jacket.

"Sorry, Sweetie. I know it's tight but it's only for a short time."

"Iow, iow."

"Mommie loves you, too."

I took my wallet from my purse and put it in the case along side of the cat and left the purse on the back seat. I turned the motor off, left the keys in the ignition and closed the door. I knew the town highway crew would bring the vehicle up the hill when they cleared the road.

Getting past the fallen tree would be the worst obstacle, or so I thought. I climbed over the stone wall, wallered through the undergrowth, back over the fence on the other side of the toppled tree. I checked my valuable cargo. Precious was cramped but all right. I brushed snow from the red jacket before I continued my trek up the hill.

Wind whipped directly into my face, pulling the attache case from my grip and sailing it to the other side of the road. My feet went out from under me. Each time I tried to get up I slid back. Apparently it had rained and frozen before it started to snow. I stayed down on the ground and crawled to Precious, dragging my left leg behind me.

The cat was crying and frightened, but unharmed from her unexpected ride through the air. I was afraid if I took her out of the case, she might try to run away. I sat on the snow-covered road and tried to comfort my four-legged companion.

Still on the ground, I slid on my backside off the road as close to the stonewall fence as I could get. The rough ground gave me better traction when I finally got back up on my feet. I held the attache case close to my body. Gusts of wind continued to sweep across my face, ice pellets stinging as they hit. I was in the middle of the hill. The lights in our house were no longer visible.

Using the high mounds of snow-covered stonewall as a guide, I turned around and made my way up the rest of the hill, backwards, holding my attache case close to my body. The snow was slippery underneath my shoes. My cane slid every time I set it down. Inch by inch I eventually came to our driveway.

Our house never looked so good. I shook the snow from the red jacket and released the cat from her confines. Muriel wiped piles of snowy icicles from my hair and clothing. The blaze from the fireplace was a welcome sight. I felt as cold as the wind sounded whistling around the corner of the house.

Precious went potty and paraded back and forth in front of the refrigerator for something to eat. The workout had given this feline an appetite. Later that evening, my companion sat on Muriel's lap and told her all about her latest adventure. She had tried to warn us that morning of the pending storm and trouble ahead.

That winter was one of the worst we ever experienced on our mountain. Muriel went back to the city for the rest of the winter. I stayed on the mountain, unable to clear our driveway, ski or do much of anything but work. The town truck dropped the plow and swung around our circle driveway. Otherwise I'd have been stranded.

Our disabilities, my helplessness and weather elements forced us to make the decision to sell our home and move into the city. It was the hardest thing Muriel and I ever had to face.

There would be no more beautiful days and nights in the special quiet of our mountain. No longer would Precious and I walk the old dirt road, watching various forms of wildlife, bears in the berry patch or beavers enjoying their private swimming pool. No more breakfasts with the deer and turkeys. No more "just the two of us" feeling the subzero calm embrace our bodies as we swished along the snow-covered fields in winter's moon-lit nights.

We said our good-byes—each in our own way. Snow-shoes cried her discontent from the cat carrier. Precious looked longingly out of the window of the Scout as we followed Muriel down the dirt road for the last time. This special cat sat on top of the back seat, surrounded by clothes and potted geraniums. My eyes were so welled with tears I could hardly see the road. Both Precious and I knew we would probably never see this beautiful place again.

CITY LIFE

When we sold our house near the Albany airport to live on our mountain, we kept a large building lot for possible future use and built a small three-bedroom ranch house on that lot.

We refused to allow the builder to cut down any trees that didn't interfere with the construction. The contractor was livid. "It will cost you more. We can't manipulate heavy equipment through that forest. We'll have to do most of the grading by hand. You'll be sorry when you are forced to pay a fortune to have these old trees removed."

"Let *us* worry about that," we said. "Leave the trees. That's final. The area you can't do with your equipment—leave that, too. We aren't sure how we want to landscape those areas anyway."

We weren't about to have our yard look like a desert with spindly twigs planted here and there. We wouldn't live long enough to see them grown to the size of the trees the builder wanted to remove.

It was harder for Muriel and me to adjust to our new surroundings than it was for our four-legged

---

friends. Snowshoes adjusted by scampering under the bed, not to be seen for three days.

Precious was busy helping unpack boxes and telling us where the furniture should go. Muriel and I thought it would be nice to put the marble-top table in front of the picture windows with a lamp on it.

"NO!" the interior decorator proclaimed. That space was reserved for her blue antique wood box, from the studio upstate, so she could soak up the warm sunshine. Her short book case would be nice next to the front door for those days when the sun was too hot. Yes, Master!

Her disappointment mounted when only one litter pan was put in the half bath. Precious growled continually because Snowshoes wasn't as neat as Precious thought she should be. Her hind feet were the cause of this untidiness. We all had a heart-to-heart talk. I told the bathroom inspector we no longer had a house the size of the Hilton. Our entire house would fit inside the recreation room of our house on the mountain. Snowshoes would try to be a little neater, and I had to promise Precious I'd do litter pan duty more often.

The cat did like the fact that I wasn't away from the house for long periods of time. Of course, this meant she didn't go on long rides. We both missed those times one on one when we would jabber back and forth during our long journeys to and from Albany.

Now we lived on a main highway with many fast-moving vehicles. It wasn't safe to let animals loose outside. Colonie has a leash law for dogs, but there is no such ordinance for cats. I continually scooped dead cats and squirrels off the pavement in front of our house.

Before we allowed Precious outside, she was fitted with a harness. The pet shop owner recommended a T-strap type. One strap went around the neck—another around her middle. The piece on top fastened the two and had a metal loop for hooking a lead.

We didn't know what to expect. The only time Precious had ever worn anything around her neck or middle was at Terry's wedding.

Precious stood perfectly still while Muriel hooked her up. It didn't phase her in the least. A small braided leash was attached to the loop. The three of us went down the back steps. Brump-brump, the cat's legs not bending.

Her former family must have trained this cat to walk on a lease. We walked around the outside of the house, up and down the driveway. Precious was an old pro. A lightweight nylon rope was secured at the car port and fastened to the leash.

Precious didn't mind being confined as long as Muriel or I were within reach. If we went to another area in the yard, we tied the rope to a concrete block or tree.

Precious spent as much time as she could with me. Whenever I went to the nursery for lawn products or to the hardware store, the cat went along. She rode the shopping cart the same as she had the lawn mower. Checkout counters backed up—everyone wanting to get a glimpse of this cute cat.

Only once did she go to a food market with me, and that was at the request of the meat department manager.

Precious had been sick. She had a fever and wouldn't eat. I called the same veterinarian from the time when we lived in Albany years before. The cat had an infection. The infection cleared up, but she still wouldn't eat. The doctor told me to try to get food into her. Anything she would eat.

I offered Fancy Feast and Sheba, but Precious wouldn't eat it. It made no difference if it was served in stemware or on a silver platter. This cat wanted no part of it. I offered tuna. That, too, was snubbed. She did find ground round to her liking. That disappeared in short order—fed in dime size pieces—*one* piece at a time. If I put several pieces in her dish she wouldn't eat it. So, ground round it was, with added vitamins and supplements to balance her diet.

She wouldn't eat just any ground round. It had to come from one particular store. I thought ground round was ground round. I guess not. But the meat had to be fresh. One day I bought a package of ground round and took it home, but the cat wouldn't eat it. The inside pieces were a gray brown. I took it back to the market and asked to speak with the meat manager.

I explained, "My little girl won't eat this. It isn't fresh, and she knows fresh meat."

The meat manager gave me a quizzical smile. "Your little girl must be very smart because she's right. This meat isn't fresh. It must have been mixed up when the meat was sorted. I'd like to meet this little girl and ask her how she can tell when meat isn't fresh. Bring your daughter in, will you?"

"I can't do that. She's a ca—" I started to explain but one of the other butchers interrupted me. He was having a problem and needed help. The meat manager started towards the meat cooler and called back, "I'll be here all afternoon. I'll expect you sometime before five. Get a refund at the customer service counter for that package you have there."

"But she's not—" I started to say again.

Too late. The big burly fellow with the hard hat disappeared into the cooler.

I went home, brought Precious back to the market, put her in a shopping cart and headed for the meat department. In back of me a male voice yelled in near panic, "You can't bring that cat in here! Animals aren't allowed!"

I stared him down saying, "The meat manager wants to see her. If she can't go back there, bring him up here. Tell him Mrs. Hine and her little girl are here."

"What do you mean—the meat manager wants to see her? Let him socialize on his own time. He knows pets aren't allowed in the store."

I agreed to go to the front of the store and wait. Several minutes later the burly fellow arrived, completely confused.

"I asked you to bring your little girl in, not your cat," he snapped.

"This *is* my little girl," I answered." I tried to tell you this morning but you were in too much of a hurry to listen."

He looked at Precious sitting in the cart as good as gold, looked at me, then at the cat again. He shook his head. "I thought cats ate anything."

"Not this cat," I said.

"You've got a spoiled brat on your hands."

"Fussy cat—yes. Good meat—no," I responded.

A crowd of shoppers huddled around us. The young messenger pushed through the crowd. "It's all right, folks. Nothing for you to be interested in. Let's break it up. You're blocking the entrance."

The butcher was embarrassed. Sheepishly he said, "I'll never live this down. My own department members can't detect poor quality meat, but a cat can."

He reached into his blood-spattered butcher's coat and pulled out a piece of paper and signed his name on the bottom." Here's a credit slip for ten dollars. Get the cat anything she wants, but please—" he hesitated, smiled. "Please—if she has any further complaints, I prefer *you* handle it—alone."

He gave Precious a pat on the head and walked to the back of the store. A small band of shoppers mulled around the checkout area wondering what was going on. One woman couldn't resist the urge to exploit the situation.

"What's that cat doing in the store? Can't you read, lady? The sign says, NO PETS ALLOWED. I'm going to call the store manager and have the food inspector brought in. Really!"

She started towards the office. I grabbed her arm. "No need to get your shorts in a bind, lady. Precious *is* the meat inspector. She forgot her hard hat today. No big deal."

I took Precious out of the cart and went to my car. I could hear laughter behind me. I'm certain that woman pondered my last remark as Precious and I drove out of the parking lot.

On the way home I asked Precious why she couldn't eat dry cat food like Snowshoes did. All I got was a dirty look.

Precious and Snowshoes weren't exactly pals-y wals-y, but each respected the other feline's feelings and territory. Snowshoes made herself scarce around humans. She was pretty much a loner.

A black and white short hair, she had been abandoned by her mother as a kitten, and she suffered from problems with her hind quarters. Her feet always gave her trouble. She was the biggest klutz I ever saw.

Two evenly marked white feet fastened to her black

body gave the illusion she wore snowshoes. Thus the name. Whenever anything was upset, torn apart or otherwise damaged, Snowshoes took the blame. With her sweet face and big green eyes she seemed to say, "Whatever it was that somebody did that you didn't want done—I didn't do it."

On occasion she came into the living room, jumped up on the TV and went to sleep, her tail hanging down across the screen.

Precious detested any obstruction to *her* viewing screen. She reprimanded the big black cat, but Snowshoes ignored the growls and howls. When all else failed, Precious jumped up, trying to catch the swinging tail. Snowshoes merely got up, turned around so her tail hung over the back of the TV. Precious was satisfied with that and took her position on my lap, gluing her eyes to the screen.

One week end my sister and a friend came to visit. They brought us a gift in a large paper shopping bag with cord handles. The bag was put in back of the TV set on the floor, and we went out to dinner. While we were gone, Snowshoes curled up on the TV.

The sound of strange voices when we arrived home sent Snowshoes scampering for cover. She jumped off the back of the TV set but instead of hitting the floor, she landed in the bag which contained the crocheted throw my sister had brought me.

The frightened cat jumped out of the bag through the handle, but her body was too big to go clear through the opening. She dragged the bag to the corner of the furniture and the wall.

"Mayday-Mayday!" Precious yowled. Just as Muriel and I got to the immobilized cat, it gave a lunge and went sailing around the corner, down the hall, bag handles and bag fragments still around her middle.

Precious ran after her housemate. Back and forth—

Snowshoes trying to get this thing off her, Precious screaming, "ERRO! ERRO!"

Snowshoes took refuge under my bed. Precious was under the bed trying to console her friend. Her big bushy tail swished back and forth by the head of the bed.

I closed the bedroom door. Muriel wrapped an old sweater around her arm and went under the bed. Talk about a cat fight. First it was Snowshoes howling and hissing. Then Precious began her spiel. In between, Muriel let out with "Ouch! I'm only trying to help!"

The bed shook. Precious came out from under the bed. I grabbed her and put her in my clothes closet. Action under the bed slowed down. Pants and wails came from behind the closet door. I heard Muriel yell, "Give me the scissors. I almost got her."

I slid the shears from the sewing table against the wall under the bed.

"There. I got it," Muriel shouted, followed by dead silence. There wasn't any noise from the closet, either. Muriel crawled out from under the bed. Precious came out of the closet. Snowshoes crouched on the floor next to the head of the bed. A week went by before she would join us in the living room. Every time she went by the TV set, Snowshoes glanced in back of it to make sure there was nothing there.

Precious enjoyed action and being with us. She always greeted us at the door when we came home.

One day she was panic stricken. We knew the howls, cries and actions all too well. Down the hall she went towards my office. Muriel and I followed. Squeezed behind my desk against the wall was Snowshoes. She didn't move. Her hind legs were stiff as boards. She had suffered a stroke.

Muriel gathered the big black and white cat up in a bath towel and went to the car. Precious wasn't about to be left behind. I put her under my arm and went down the back steps. During the entire examination, Precious pranced back and forth in the doctor's waiting room like an expectant father. The doctor thought he might be able to do something for the sick cat, but it could be costly. Did we want to incur the expense?

"Do whatever is necessary," I told him.

Muriel and I wondered if the excitement of the bag handle incident might have triggered the stroke.

The doctor assured us such was not the case. "She's getting on in years. This frequently happens. We might be able to get her walking again. We'll know more in a couple of days. Give me a call then."

We gave Snowshoes a kiss. Precious extended an "iow." The sick cat's green eyes blinked but were not clear and sparkling as they normally were.

It was a long wait. The call brought good news, but we couldn't take Snowshoes home until Saturday. Precious was usually very receptive to hugs and kisses from the folks at the hospital. Not that Saturday. She was only interested in seeing her friend. We heard voices coming down the hall. Precious perked her ears. Her body trembled. Snowshoes was put down on the floor.

"Go see your Mommie," the kindly voice told her. The cat didn't come to me. She went to her long-haired furry friend instead.

The two cats moved towards each other, kissed, hissed, rolled over and then sat staring into the other's eyes, with the expression, "Why are we doing this? We don't really like each other that much."

Snowshoes went into the carrying case. I tucked Precious under my arm. The doctor spoke to all of us. "Snowshoes had a mini stroke. We've worked on her hind legs, but they must have been injured before."

I explained her ailments as a kitten.

Simply Precious   83

"That explains some of her problem. It's important she exercise. Going up and down stairs is the best therapy. Give her this medicine, too."

Of course Precious understood every word the doctor said. She went to nursing at once. Snowshoes was groggy the first few days. She didn't move from her bed except to eat and go potty. The nurse didn't fuss when her sick friend missed the litter pan. The bathroom inspector simply ordered me to clean it up.

Snowshoes's nurse had lots of experience with recovery programs. To get the sick cat to move, Precious kept nudging her while talking to her. (Animals have a language all their own. I didn't understand a word of it.)

Eventually, the patient followed Precious up and down the hall but wouldn't go near the open cellar door. She never traveled those steps. Snowshoes stood at the top of the steps while Precious brumped down the wood treads.

Once on the cellar floor Precious turned, looked up, rattled off something, which I suppose meant "Come on. You can do it."

Snowshoes turned and high-tailed it back to the bedroom, Precious in hot pursuit. There was no escaping this determined little vixen. She had viewed enough television to know how to corral the critter.

"EIOW!"

The patient slinked behind the therapist to the open cellar doorway. Together they brumped down the stairs. A couple of minutes later two faces appeared at the top landing. Up and down, up and down, morning and night for two months. Precious was in her glory. She had someone to care for. It was the same routine as when Muriel and I required her assistance. Eating, going potty and sleeping.

When Snowshoes curled up to take a nap, Precious tried to get as close to her patient as possible. Most of the time she ended up on top of her sick friend. Snowshoes didn't complain. The two cats became good buddies.

It was a good time for Muriel and me. We had time to do things that needed to be done around the house *our way*. Precious was too preoccupied to notice.

One night, three years later, we came home after dinner and a show. Precious wasn't at the door to greet us. We called to her, but she still didn't come. Muriel heard that familiar cry. We switched on all the lights and began to search.

Precious was in back of the sofa staring up at Muriel. Her mournful cry sent shivers up our backs. The cat was sitting next to her fur-covered friend. Snowshoes didn't move. She had suffered a fatal stroke.

Our beloved Snowshoes was put to rest in the back yard. The next three days there was no living with Precious.

She pulled and squirmed at the end of her lead rope. Muriel moved her rope near the dead cat's grave. All day long, in the heat of early fall, Precious refused to leave the pile of dirt. She stretched out across the grave, her head resting on her front paws—just staring at the dirt beneath her. She wouldn't eat.

When we brought her in at dark, she carried on by the back door. She scratched and whined for hours. The next morning Precious was still at the door waiting to go out and be with the deceased animal. I never realized animals grieve losses the same as humans.

Simply Precious

Precious was now alone. There were no other fur-covered house residents. The cat had to be content with Reggie, our pet squirrel, and Chippy the Chipmunk. The chipmunk took pleasure in tantalizing the cat and making her life miserable.

Precious's lead cord was fastened to the carport post. It gave her access to cover if it rained as well as to flower beds, shrubs and the back porch. One of her favorite spots was on top of an old wine keg next to the back porch steps.

We originally bought the keg for a rain barrel, but before we had a chance to knock the top out, Precious claimed the barrel for her own. The stopper would never stay put in the bung hole. It kept popping out. Chippy played in the barrel. It's a wonder the wine fumes didn't make him high—or maybe they did.

He went in and out of the hole, up and around the sides of the barrel. One day he scrambled up the outside of the barrel, started across the top and came face to face with two big yellow eyes. Precious took a swing with a paw, but Chippy was too fast. The cat got up, stretched her neck over the side of the barrel, lost her balance and fell to the ground. Chippy thought this was hilarious. He sat up—out of cat's reach—chitter chattered—ran in and out of the barrel. In and out under the back porch stairs. His tail stood straight up as his sleek tan body with black stripes scurried to and fro.

Precious tried to follow the route this little tease took but got hung up on the porch railing. I heard, "ERRO, ERRO!" She was hanging off the porch, suspended by the lead cord like a bag of clothespins on a pulley line.

Chippy vanished while I rescued my furry friend. The rope once more untangled stretched its full length. Just beyond the reach of the cat sat Chippy. "Chitter chatter—chitter chatter." He dared Precious to try and catch him.

One day Chippy got careless. He sneaked up on the barrel where Precious was stretched out, supposedly napping in the warm October sun. All of a sudden—WHAM!— she got him. I rushed to Chippy's aide. Instead of attacking the chipmunk like most cats would, Precious had her front paw on the little animal's body while she licked the little tease's face. When I yelled, "Precious! Let go," the cat jumped off the barrel. Chippy scurried under the porch.

This cat had no killer instinct. She just wanted to play. Ferninand of the felines. Chipmunks continue to occupy much of Precious's time when she's outside.

Squirrels have somewhat different attitudes. Most are afraid of anything that moves. There is one exception. Reggie.

He comes to the kitchen door every morning for his goodies. He waits on the porch railing while I shell peanuts. He doesn't like them with the shells on. He knows, too, that I always have peanuts in my pocket.

I hang my jacket on the back of the lawn chair and watch while Reggie stands on his hind legs and sticks his nose into the pocket.

The squirrel keeps his distance from Precious. Apparently this rodent measured the cat's lead cord. Precious stretches out on the lawn. Reggie bounces by, the cat gives him a dirty look and flops her head back down on the grass. These two animals were a big help when Muriel and I planted bulbs. Precious helped dig holes to drop the bulbs into.

Reggie must not have liked the way we did it because he proceeded to dig the bulbs up and transplant them elsewhere. He worked long and hard at this project. I didn't have the heart to tell him his eye for color wasn't as good as Precious's. Reggie and Precious must have sworn a secret pact not to invade each

---

Simply Precious 87

other's territory. The squirrel uses any area of the yard Precious's lead cord doesn't reach.

We were not as lucky with other animals that sometimes roam on our property. It is fair to assume that if you have a pet tied outside, he/she will be safe. Right? Not at all. You just can't secure your pet outside and not keep careful watch over it.

Precious was in the back yard. I was in the kitchen. I heard a sound that resembled heavy breathing like a horse in full gallop. A howl, a bark, a rustle of dirt and gravel scratching and a loud thump brought me to the kitchen door to see where Precious was. She was nowhere to be seen. However, there was a big German Shepherd dog pouncing up against my car in the carport.

I grabbed a straw broom as I started down the stairs. Precious had managed to jump up on the carport's ledge between the flower pots and was on top of my station wagon, her lead stretched as far as it could go.

A long chain fastened to the dog's collar was tangled around the post of the back steps. At the other end was a cork screw anchor. The dog had pulled the anchor out of the ground and dragged it with him from the row of houses in back of our property. How he managed to travel that distance between shrubs, fences and trees without getting hung up, was a mystery.

The dog came to me when I spoke to him. There were no name tags or license tags on the collar. I called the animal control center. Muriel lifted Precious down from the luggage rack of the Subaru and went inside. I retrieved an old chain link leash from the cellar, snapped it on the frightened dog's collar and gave him a dish of water.

An hour passed before the animal control vehicle arrived—with a young girl the single occupant. I offered to walk the dog to the back of the van, but she insisted on removing the leash and replacing it with her noose type.

"He's going to slip that lead," I told her. "Take my leash. It belonged to my Dalmation. You can bring it back later."

"He'll be all right. I've done this hundreds of times," she replied. Three steps towards the open van door and the Shepherd slipped the noose and ran down through our back yard.

I walked to the van, ready to get in. "Come on," I motioned. "We can catch him on the back street." The girl shrugged her shoulders. "Forget it. That's one less I have to worry about." She drove down the driveway. I went inside and filed a complaint with animal control.

The dog must have found his way home because three days later he was back, this time attacking Thunder, the black Labrador who lived next door. Thunder was always tied except when he and his owner visited with us.

Muriel heard the dogs fighting. She ran down the back steps, picked up the bucket of water we leave there for flowers, and started across the yard. She threw the water on the two dogs.

Thunder tried to back down, but the Shepherd had him down, his chain taut. The black lab freed himself and ran to Muriel for protection, the intruder hot on his heels. Thunder circled Muriel. His chain wrapped around her legs and upset her. Muriel was being trampled under eight legs, the chain pulling tighter and tighter around her ankle.

I turned on the garden hose and headed for the scuffle. The hose didn't phase either fighter. They still went at each other. Muriel was yelling, "My leg! My leg!" I took my cane and tried to hook into Thunder's chain. I missed. I pushed the cane at the Shepherd while I unhooked Thunder's lead. Now Thunder was loose.

I rushed to Muriel. The dogs continued their scrimmage some distance away. The chain had broken the skin and cut into the flesh. The leg looked bad. Muriel let out a whoop as I removed the links from her ankle.

Out of nowhere we saw a black and white object zoom past us and land on the Shepherd's head. It was Precious. She must have sneaked out of the back door behind me and waited for the chance to pounce.

I was on the ground with Muriel. The two dogs were still going at each other, with the cat trying to hang on to her position on the Shepherd's head. The way the dogs were flouncing around, Precious was sure to get killed. The cat was thrown to the ground. She jumped right back up on the intruder's head.

Suddenly, the Shepherd let out a yelp and shook his head furiously. Blood streamed down over his eyes and muzzle. The cat had glommed the dog's face and forehead. The cat hung on as the dog tried to shake her loose. Her front claws dug deeper. The Shepherd made a beeline for the back yard. The black and white fur ball bounced back and forth on his head between his ears.

The dog stopped, shook his head vigorously. This time the cat flew into orbit. The dog continued to run down through the back yard, yapping all the way. Precious wasn't hurt. She watched the big bully disappear behind the neighbor's fence. She slowly started to walk back to her friends, stopped, looked behind her to make sure the intruder didn't return.

I went to the cat. She was OK. I was, too, but Muriel and Thunder needed medical attention. The wounded were evacuated to our house. Thunder had small bites and two big holes in his side. He would be all right.

What about our human friend who got "wrapped up

in her work"? Her leg was no joking matter. I applied ice packs. Her leg was black and blue from the ankle to her knee. The chain links formed a pattern around the broken skin. She refused to go to the emergency room. My first aid kit serviced both dog and human.

Thunder's owners weren't home at the time. They had gone shopping. Neighbors next to them saw the entire thing and told us they "didn't want to get involved." The Shepherd never came around again. I do believe Precious saved the day for all of us, to say nothing of revenging the dog's invasion of her privacy three days earlier. Her big, black bushy tail stood straight up as she strutted like a turkey gobbler while she jawed and jabbered. She was telling us, "Nobody messes with my friends unless they want trouble."

From that day forward Precious was not allowed outside unless someone was with her. She had to wait until I'd finished all my inside chores so I could be with her.

The only time Precious didn't object to being inside was when Muriel and I worked on our crafts. Muriel does needle work, counted cross stitch, samplers and button and bow type crafts. I make wood clocks, inlaid pictures and novelty wood items for our craft shows and custom orders.

Precious helps Muriel straighten (?) yarn and thread needles as well as choose colors to be used on various projects.

She prefers to help me with wood. There's more action in it. The cat isn't allowed in my shop when I use the table saw or other dangerous equipment. She does help with scroll saw cutting, drilling, sanding and painting.

The scroll saw and small drill press sit on a large

work bench. Precious finds a spot in back of the equipment, and supervises at a safe distance. The vibration of the saw, noise and flying sawdust don't bother her. Sometimes she is white with sawdust. Weather permitting, we take the cut pieces of wood outside to clean. I have less interference from my helper when we are in the carport. When we are in the house, Precious feels she should be on top of my work, in my pocket if she could manage.

I keep telling her the big bushy tail is too coarse a brush for my fine work but she pays no attention. She throws herself into her work and ends up looking like a rainbow. She does have a good eye for color.

We made a trip to a paint manufacturer in Massachusetts when that company featured a new line of craft paints. It was a stifling hot day in July. Muriel went, into the showroom while Precious and I stayed in the car, the air conditioner running full blast. Minutes later Muriel appeared at the showroom doorway, waving me inside.

"What about Precious?" I asked.

"They said to bring her with you. They love cats," was her reply.

The reception area was filled with beautiful figurines and other wares that demonstrated the many uses this new product offered. One nudge of the face or swish of the tail meant trouble, especially since there was a sign displayed, **"YOU BREAK IT, YOU BUY IT."** Oh, boy.

We weaved through the minefield of niceties to the conference room. Precious walked slowly on her leash while I held my breath. We were greeted by two gracious ladies.

My inquisitive four-legged friend was anxious to see what these new paints were, too. After all, she'd traveled for hours to get to this place. She sat on the floor, voicing her displeasure. One of the sales ladies stopped her demonstration, brought two cardboard boxes from a back room and placed them on the chair at the head of the table.

"Will she mind if I pick her up and put her on the boxes?" she asked.

I shook my head, No, and the cat took her place at the head of the table. She sat motionless, her eyes drawn to the brushes as the demonstration continued. Our biggest problem was making our selection. There were so many colors and textures to choose from.

One sales lady asked, "What does our little four-legged artist friend think? Come on Precious, help us out here." I thought the woman was out of her mind when she motioned for the cat to get up on the table.

Our color specialist hopped onto the table and walked over to the jars. She sniffed, walked to and from, sniffed again. Time out. She had to scratch. All paint containers were examined again. Her head went forward, pushed certain jars, ignoring others. One hostess laughed. "I think Precious is trying to tell you which ones you should take," she said as she turned to the woman with her.

"I've never seen anything like this. Have you?"

The other woman shook her head saying, "Are you sure this is a cat? I don't believe my eyes."

Precious continued to study her selection. She pushed the jars she wanted out of the lineup. Once her decision was made, she went back to her seat at the head of the table. Her smug glances told us, "There—that wasn't so complicated, was it?"

The order was written up and we were on our way. As we were about to get into the car, one lady called, "Let us know if the top cat made the right choices." She hugged Precious and softly remarked, "You know, don't you, no one is ever going to believe this. We should have taken pictures. This cat is simply Precious." She chuckled and added, "She certainly was given the right name."

The paint was a huge success. Well, almost. The purple paint sat around until Barney became popular with the kids. The orange was so bright you had to wear sunglasses in order to stay in the same room with it. It took your breath away. It finally was consumed at Halloween three years later.

Precious never cared much for the executive branch of our business. We never told her she did a good job of selecting paint. There would be no living with her. She preferred to do more worthwhile things like unraveling Muriel's needlework, or pushing cotton pompons. Best of all, she loved to help me glue my wood inlaid pictures and other craft items.

Glue had the same effect on her as catnip. Her head was always in the glue can whenever glue was used. It may sound like fun, but YOU try getting that sticky stuff off a long-hair fur ball. It's like chewing gum on your shoes. Thank goodness, that brand of glue could be removed with soap and water while it was still wet. Let it dry and you needed a chisel.

The telephone rang as I opened the can of glue. I rested the lid on top of the can and left my work table. Precious was sniffing the lid. A half hour later, when I returned, the cat was lying on the plywood press boards. She didn't move as I dipped the brush into the glue and spread the thick mixture on the back of the picture.

I thought it odd she didn't get up but paid little attention until I reached for the board she was on. She didn't get off. Fact is, she couldn't. Her long fur was glued to the board. She had knocked the lid off the can and rolled on it while I was out of the room

The only way I could release her body was to use the scissors. She hadn't had such a haircut since she first came to live with us. Her entire left side looked like a moth-eaten fur collar.

Inlaid pictures of her likeness hang in homes and offices from Maine to Florida. No one fully understands the torment she went through posing and making these works of art. Not one of the pictures has her personal autograph of black fur stuck to the back. The press board does, though.

Precious let it be known she was very unhappy with the setup that she could not join us at craft shows. After all—she worked hard to help make these crafts. The least we could do is let her help sell them.

One wood item was Rudy, a deer twenty inches long and fifteen inches wide, with big cow eyes. I set Rudy on Precious's wood box to dry. The cat examined the motionless body, nuzzled up against it and went to sleep. To this cat, the deer was another sibling to nurture. Brown paint was all over black fur.

Muriel and I thought it so cute the way the cat stayed with the wood deer that we left Rudy on the wood box until the morning of the show. Most of our crafts were packed in computer paper boxes. They're just a nice size to handle, and they have lids. Rudy's antlers prohibited our putting a lid on his box. We wrapped him in tissue, stuffed loose newspapers around him and set the box by the door to be loaded last.

As usual, we were running late. Muriel checked the kitchen to make sure we hadn't forgotten anything. She set the house alarm and pulled the door closed. Setting up shows is hustle bustle. People coming and going. I set up the tables while Muriel brought the rest of the boxes in. The show opened at ten o'clock, but a lot of lookers hovered around some of the tables well ahead of opening time.

Since Rudy was a new item to our line, we made a special place for him. He would come out of his box last. I noticed people coming by our display laughing and reaching down towards Rudy. I knew he was cute, but not *that* cute. If potential customers were that interested in this deer, I'd better put him on display now.

I reached down to take Rudy from his box. It wasn't the deer that drew their attention. Peering through the crushed newspapers around the deer's head was a black and white head with big yellow eyes. Precious!

She had buried herself in the box while it sat on the kitchen floor waiting to be loaded. Muriel panicked. The cat knew I was annoyed but she looked so cute sitting there, head moving back and forth, rubbing her neck against Rudy's head that I didn't have the heart to scold her.

We took a nylon cord from the glove compartment and secured it around the cat's neck. The other end we anchored under a folding chair behind our booth. When we loaded the boxes that morning we had removed the bag of litter and the water dish that we usually kept in the wagon. A nearby convenience store sold small bags of litter. A box lid served as a pan and was put under the table. A styrofoam cup was her water dish.

Precious wasn't satisfied she had completely disrupted our day. She didn't want to be *under* the table. She wanted to be with Rudy *on* the table. There was no living with her. The cat carried on so that she drew attention of crafters and customers alike. I'm sure everyone thought I was beating this animal to death.

We changed the display to accommodate the stowaway. At first people were so enthralled with the cat that they hardly noticed Rudy. The cat plopped herself down in front of the wood ornament, curled up and stuck her face into the mass of long black fur.

Whenever someone remarked about Rudy's cute face and eyes, two yellow eyes poked through the black and white fur mass. We made a sign and attached it to the deer:

**WILL TAKE ORDERS. SORRY THE
CAT DOESN'T GO WITH IT.**

The only time Precious moved from the display was lunch time. She didn't like my peanut butter sandwiches or Muriel's ham and cheese. We paid two dollars and fifty cents for a hamburger from the concession stand, knowing full well she wouldn't eat it because it wasn't ground round. She got no sympathy from me. Tough darts! That's the price she'd have to pay for stowing away without preparing herself for the duration of her journey. Maybe if she got hungry enough she'd think twice before she horned in where not invited or prepared to handle. This feline took the scolding like a trooper, jumped back up on the display and joined her friend.

Sales of Rudy were booming. There were times during the day when I considered giving the cat away.

From that day on, the last thing we checked before going to a craft show was, *"Where's Precious?"*

Through the years I've tried to tell myself nothing Precious ever does is with malicious intent. She merely wants to be helpful and feel needed. Mother's little helper always has to be in the middle of the action.

After my retirement I began a second career of writing. With a cat curled up in my lap, I managed to get through a writing course and started to write my first book. Precious was lonely because I spent so much time at my typewriter and didn't pay much attention to her. If Mohammed won't go to the mountain. . . You know the rest.

At first she was content to clear a space on my desk near the typewriter. And I do mean clear. Anything in her way kept inching to the edge of the desk until it fell off. I do my typing on an old Royal manual typewriter. The cat was fascinated by my hands moving, keys striking and the carriage return. She stared at the machine and movement. That soon became boring. How much more fun it would be to catch the keys. In order to do this she had to move over on the typewriter stand.

I raised the dropleaf to give the typing critic the required space to do her job more efficiently. Getting clipped by the keys a few times must have smarted because she decided to rest on the typing stand until it came time to proofread.

It's a good thing the pages were numbered. This little rascal waited until my back was turned, then plowed into the pile of typed sheets, sending them flying to the floor. She particularly enjoyed pushing the highlighter as I made corrections for my editor. The first set of galleys resembled a drunken sailor trying to walk a straight line. The markers brought back the days she helped Terry and me in the office. I put explanations in the margins and extended my apologies for not being able to draw a straight line with a ruler. Proofreading was limited to times when Precious slept or was occupied elsewhere with Muriel. She didn't falter in her efforts to help me complete that manuscript. She bounced through seventy thousand words while hanging on the typewriter stand. Precious's name appears in the acknowledgments of that manuscript.

After giving complete dedication to our work, Precious deserved a vacation. We all took a break and went on a trip to visit Muriel's elderly aunt, a resident in a nursing facility in Pennsylvania. We had been at the nursing home for several hours. I went to the car to check on the cat. I took her for a walk in and around one of the many courtyards at the facility. We were enjoying the early May sunshine when a social worker came out to talk with me.

"What a beautiful cat. Is she friendly?" she asked.

"Friendly? She loves everybody," I answered.

"Would you like to visit with some of our residents? So many of our guests long for their pets. We encourage people who visit to bring their pets along as long as they are well behaved."

Precious was raring to go. The young lady looked at the cat. "I've never seen a cat walk on a leash. Was it difficult teaching her to do that?"

"No, I think her previous owners taught her. She was a seasoned walker when we got her," I replied."

"It's amazing. Remarkable. Simply precious. What's her name?"

"Precious," I answered. "No other name even crossed our minds when we named her."

"You can leave her with me while you continue your trip," she said.

"Fat chance. She's our navigator. We'll be happy to visit, though, won't we Precious?"

We followed the social worker into the building. Everyone was in awe to see a cat strut down halls on a leash. I was apprehensive about exposing Precious to sick and older people. I didn't know how she would react. I soon found out. She didn't care that they picked her up from the wrong end or left her head dangling somewhere in the middle. Hugs and kisses more than compensated for the cat's uncomfortable position. She never extended her claws or tried to get away. She just stayed put until everyone finished making a fuss over her.

Every time we visited with Aunt B we stopped at the reception desk to announce our arrival. One day a new face was at the front desk. "May I tell Miss Morgan who's calling?"

"Oh, just tell her Precious is here," I said.

"So this is Precious! I've heard so much about this cat. Hello, kitty. You make everyone so happy when you visit."

Precious wasn't at all impressed with her celebrity status. She stretched out on the deep piled carpet and waited for her friend.

We never gave much thought to use of animals in therapy for the aging until we went to Aunt B's nursing home. This cat's keen perception and disposition made her an ideal candidate for such work. Social work became Precious's new career. We made our rounds to other adult homes. Residents had an entirely different attitude while we were there. They may not remember *my* name, but when they see the cat walk down the corridors on a leash, they chime, "Here comes Precious."

They flock around this animal like kids around an ice cream truck. Those who can walk shuffle down the hall to be with this celebrity. Wheelchairs do a turn-around hoping they won't be too late to see the cat. A blind woman caresses Precious's long silky fur. Tears of joy roll down the old woman's face as she recalls her own cats of years gone by. Residents who are mobile are thrilled to take the cat's leash and go for a walk down the hall. Precious walks ever so slowly so as not to tug at her lead.

We don't limit our visits to just nursing homes. There are many lonely shut-ins who long for anyone's company, especially an animal. Chances are at some time in their lives they have had a cat or a dog. These lonely shut-ins look forward to our visits.

Homes, once unkempt, are now clean and orderly when we arrive. Personal hygiene has also improved together with alertness of mind. Precious stays on the floor unless invited to sit on a lap and be rocked. She loves to be rocked. I suppose it's because of her many hours of rocking as a young sick cat.

"Grandmas" offer treats which are gently taken from gnarled arthritic lands. This cat has manners. She eats things offered to her which she wouldn't eat at home. The cat brings small gifts, sometimes fastened to her harness and helps unwrap them, to the recipient's delight.

One woman is confined to bed but insists the cat join her. Precious stays on the woman's stomach under the covers, while they jabber all afternoon about the topics of the day.

Her love for children is eminent. I'm sure her original home had children. Our neighbors never had to look far for their kids. They were always in our yard playing with Precious.

One of the cat's little playmates was diagnosed with a tumor and was sent to a children's hospital in New England. We went to visit him. We thought we would have to leave Precious at the motel, but the hospital welcomed pets. Many youngsters were terminally ill, but all were excited when we arrived. Children romped in the recreation area. Precious modeled clothes, rode in a wagon and knocked down blocks. Patients confined to bed received special visits.

After an afternoon at the hospital, we returned to our motel. Precious was restless. Muriel and I knew something was going on, mentally, with this cat.

"I'll take her for a walk," Muriel said and put the blue harness on the cat. Precious pulled at her leash. "Calm down," Muriel told her four-legged friend. "We both need some air."

"I'll wait for you in the lobby. My legs have just about had it for today," I told Muriel. The desk clerk saw Muriel and Precious leave the building. The telephone rang. The young lady behind the desk called to me. "Precious has a phone call."

"What?" I answered as I started across the room.

"Precious has a phone call," she repeated. "It sounds urgent."

In the excitement, the hospital attendant had forgotten my name but knew the name of my four-legged companion. Kevin Babcock, a critically ill patient, had taken a turn for the worse and had asked for Precious. An eerie feeling enveloped me once more. Precious knew something was wrong.

Kevin smiled when we walked into his room. Precious went to his outstretched arms, snuggled down, resting her head next to his chin. For over an hour, the boy stroked her back while she looked into his face, purring her contentment. The strokes stopped. The small thin hand went limp. Precious nudged Kevin's hand but it didn't move. Her head pushed his hand again. It still didn't move.

She glanced our way, gave the boy a nudge with her head, wiggled from his body and came to me. She knew her special friend was gone. Kevin's mother went to the boy's bed. We stood outside the hospital room door to allow Mrs. Babcock some privacy in her initial moments of grief. Choked with emotion, Kevin's mother approached us.

"Kevin talked of nothing but Precious these past two days. Thank you for making his last moments such happy ones."

Precious was quiet. Her body trembled. Mrs. Babcock scratched my companion's ears, adding, "This little girl is simply precious." Muriel and I burst into tears. A young woman had just lost her son, yet she was thanking Precious for being there. The cat was a comfort to a stranger, even in death.

The jingle of car keys brings our gadabout to her feet and to the door, ready to go. It doesn't have to be to Maine or Pennsylvania. It doesn't matter if it's for a week or an hour. If we haven't planned any long over-night trips, Precious is content to go down to Ann Lee Pond by the Albany Airport and feed the ducks and geese.

In late spring and early summer water fowl can be counted by the dozens. The geese are quite tame but are still protective of their young. Precious was familiar with quail up on our mountain. The baby birds held a familiar shape to her.

I held her leash tight, but the cat kept pulling while eyeing the young brown birds pecking the cracked corn in the grass. I sat down on a bench and threw bread to the mallards and geese. Precious kept her eyes glued to the chicks.

Without warning, Papa goose flew into the cat, chasing her under the bench. The big bird stood in front of the bench, honking, his head and neck moving in and out, his wings flapping vigorously. Precious was shaking in her pantaloons. I picked her up, tried to comfort her, but she wouldn't get off my lap.

On our next visit the cat stayed close to my legs, cautiously peering around them to see if anything or anyone was lurking around the corner of the bench. The sight of a goose and Precious was under the bench or on my lap. Papa goose did some surveying himself to make sure his offspring didn't wander into the path of the furry stalker.

These two very different creatures soon made peace with each other. The goose honked, the cat RROWed, and I acted as mediator. We placed feed a safe distance from our bench, and Precious respected the feathered families' territory.

Regardless of where you travel, there is always added preparation to make sure your pet will be properly cared for while you're gone. We are fortunate in that Precious loves to ride. She always goes with us.

As soon as we put our luggage on the twin bed, Precious knows she's going someplace. She paces back and forth to the closet until her travel case appears alongside ours. Yes—this feline has her own luggage, a bright blue plastic insulated carrying case about the size of a six pack. Letters— PET ON THE GO—together with paw prints, decorate the sides. Anyone who travels with a pet should have one of these handy cases. Several mail order houses feature them.

There is a bottle for water, a covered container, water and food dishes and an envelope type compartment on the attached zippered lid. Her papers on vaccinations, etc. are kept in there. A twenty-foot lead cord, brush, comb, Tender Vittles and three cans of cat food are always left in the case. We also include a spoon, knife and fork. (No, the cat doesn't use them. We do, for spooning and cutting her food. Precious is smart, but not *that* smart.) Just before we leave the house, we add frozen ground round and ice packs.

A tote bag with Mickey Mouse's picture on it holds the cat's sheet, blanket, towel and pillow. The tote bag was a gift from Terry after her honeymoon trip to Disney World.

It takes about a week to pack our suitcases. Without permission, she hops onto the bed and sits in the middle of the open luggage. She obviously doesn't consider luggage furniture.

We spread our cosmetics, underwear and other clothing on the bed waiting for the cat to leave. As soon as she vacates her post, we rush to shift the items to the bag and close it. Precious follows the bellhop, usually Muriel, back and forth to the back door. I swear this cat can count. Once all the bags are by the door, she is impatient to get her harness on and go to the car.

One of the back seats of the station wagon is folded down. The litter pan and water dish go into the cargo area. Next comes the PET ON THE GO case and Mickey Mouse. The old red jacket is spread across the other back seat. Precious gets into the car, curls down and pretends to be asleep.

We could spend the next hour packing the rest of our things and the cat would never move. We firmly believe she does this deliberately so she doesn't have to tip the bellhop. Once the car is in motion, the tight-wad slinks over into the front seat onto my lap.

We make our travel plans far in advance to accommodate our fur-covered companion. Not all motels accept pets. Those that do usually allow small pets to stay free. Others charge from three to ten dollars a night.

One motel in Kentucky had a big sign on their front window—"Of course we welcome pets. If they will guarantee that you won't stop up the sink, leave water running, burn holes in the carpet or take our towels, you can stay, too." Ha! I like their thinking.

Only once were we deprived lodging because of Precious. For reasons that had nothing to do with Precious, we had to cut our vacation short and headed home two days early. We canceled our reservations and zipped north along Route 81. Motel signs reared above the tree-lined landscape. Off and on—off and on the highway we drove. There was a religious convention in Virginia. All motels were either full or had posted a notice: **NO PETS ALLOWED.**

It was almost midnight. I told my four-legged companion it was all her fault and we were destined to spend the night in the back seat of the station wagon if the next motel didn't have a room for us. She was unconcerned. It was her way of punishing me for cutting her vacation short. Muriel stopped in front of the motel entrance. "Oh, no!" she said, sounding exhausted. We saw the all-too familiar sign—NO PETS ALLOWED fastened to the door. The neon sign above flashed VACANCY.

"What do you think?" she asked. "Think we can sneak fuzzy Britches in?"

"Anything's worth a try," I answered. "I can't see straight, let alone drive any further."

I made small talk as I signed the register. The freckle-faced man handed me a key and went back to his TV program. Muriel carried our bags to the room, returned for Precious's litter pan and luggage camouflaged with a sheet wrapped around them. So far so good. . .

Precious waited in the car. Muriel told her to remain quiet until they reached our room. The cat had no problem with that. Muriel wrapped Precious in her old red jacket and started through the lobby. The elevator was a few yards away.

Suddenly a man's voice blared. "Excuse me, Madam." Muriel's head turned and saw the desk clerk stretching his neck around the corner of the partition. Again he said, "Excuse me. Checkout time is normally 10:30 a.m. However, I strongly suggest you and your red jacket with the bushy black lining hanging out be gone before the morning shift comes on at 8 a.m., or we're all in trouble."

He pointed to the jacket. Precious's tail had slipped out from under the jacket and was swinging back and forth. Without another word, he smiled, gave Muriel a wink and went back to the television program.

We had everything packed into the car by 7 a.m. without further incident. I returned to the front desk, smiled at the freckled face and handed him an envelope with the room key. Inside the envelope was a note and a ten dollar bill. The note read, "I'll make sure to check the lining in my red jacket before I venture out again. Thanks a million. You were a lifesaver."

Virginia has more conventions than any other state we've visited. We were in Roanoke on business. There was a convention at the motel where we stayed. Our appointment was for 10 a.m. downtown.

Muriel and Precious went for their usual morning walk before we left for our meeting. No one was in the meeting room when cat and friend strolled by and went outside. On the way back, people clustered in and around the convention center entrance.

All heads turned as Precious and Muriel approached. Muriel found herself in the meeting room, people flocking around the cat. A large-framed man in a dark suit tried to call the meeting to order but everyone ignored him. They continued to talk with the two intruders. Room service wheeled in carts of coffee and

Danish. An older man asked Muriel to join him for breakfast.

Muriel explained she was due downtown by 10 a.m. and had to leave. She thanked him, picked Precious up and walked towards the door.

The man in the dark suit pounded the gavel. "Will this meeting *please* come to order."

The microphone on the podium was on, so we all heard as he spoke softly to the younger man beside him. "I hope her meeting starts better than this, one. Whoever she's seeing better be prepared to spend time with that cat. Better still, he might have brains enough to keep the cat out of the room."

Muriel couldn't resist. She turned around and called out, "I'm sorry we interrupted your day. The people we're meeting with *expect* Precious to attend. She's our purchasing agent." The entire room exploded with laughter. The door opened and swung back and forth as Muriel and her four-legged business partner disappeared.

Precious draws a crowd wherever she goes. Our destination on one trip was Daytona Beach, Florida. We arrived early at our overnight stop in Savannah, Georgia. This was our first visit to this fascinating city, saturated in history. Literature on the table in our room told of the city's highlights The city was made up of squares—each one with its own story to tell.

An asterisk on the map indicated where our motel was located in conjunction with the walking tours along brick and cobblestone paved streets. It was spring. Azaleas and other shrubs and plants were in full bloom.

Maps in hand, we began our stroll. Our fur-covered friend was on her leash. A fountain spurting water fascinated the cat. She watched the water shoot into the air then fall into the round pool below. A wooden bench next to a brick path beckoned us.

We sat soaking up the warm spring sunshine, enjoying the splendor of the beauty around us. Spanish moss hung gracefully from the oak branches. Tall black iron fences encompassed manicured yards. Horse-drawn carriages clip-clopped up the cobblestone street.

Precious made herself comfortable in the middle of the path. She stretched out, her long fur moving gently in the breeze. A group of about fifteen people moved towards us. They were part of one of the many walking tours promoted by the city. The cat didn't move. Before I could pick her up, the tour group was on top of us.

One woman rushed forward. "My God. What's wrong with the cat? Is it dead?"

The tour guide was annoyed. He had been going through his spiel about Oglethorpe setting up camp on this very spot, when he was rudely interrupted—by a cat no less. (It wasn't Precious's fault. She was just stretching her legs, resting and enjoying the breeze.)

Members of the tour ignored the guide and gathered around the cat. Precious was now up and moving between legs. Since she couldn't rest in peace, she apparently decided she might just as well join the crowd. Women asked questions and told stories of their own pets.

"Let's keep moving. We're running behind schedule," the guide injected into the chitchat. The crowd paid no attention. They continued to discuss animals. Precious was hugged and kissed as tourists passed her from one person to another. The guide once again began his narration. This time in a high, irritated tone. "As I said before this animal crossed our path, this is where Oglethorpe set up camp when he first came into Savannah. He and his troops camped here until the first settlement was built." (I don't know how true that statement is, but that's what he told us.)

"Are there any questions?" he asked.

A six-year-old girl looked puzzled. "Yes, sir," she called out. "Why did Mr. Ogla-Orgl-Oglethorpe set up a camp site? Why didn't he go check into that there motel?" She pointed to the large motel complex directly in back of them, where we were staying. Everyone except the guide roared.

"There weren't any buildings here then," was all he said. "Let's keep moving. We are one half hour behind schedule."

Precious's new friends took pictures, said their good-byes and went on their way. We strolled for another hour before we realized how far we had walked. My legs were killing me, and the cat wanted to be carried.

The area we were in was also a "Trolley Tram Stop." With Precious under her arm, Muriel stepped into the tram. I followed. The driver-guide was sensitive to our furry companion. Every time we stopped, while tourists went into buildings, Precious, the driver and I remained in the vehicle. Every "Pet Walk" area we came to, I was asked if the cat had to go potty.

I didn't dare tell the young lady Precious only uses her own toilet. She would never dream of backing up against a bush in the wide open spaces. Even when at home and outside, this cat insists on being let inside to go to the bathroom. She goes—I wait—then it's right back outside again.

We viewed more "squares" before we started down a steep cobblestone street lined with high stone walls to the river front. Almost everyone took leave of the tram to venture along Market Square and the tourist shopping section of the city. We were allowed to board another tram any time before 8 p.m.

The waterfront was beautiful. The entire area was terraced in brick with raised planter boxes exploding with bright colored plants. Muriel bought each of us an ice cream cone. We sat on a bench, watched a paddle boat come into dock, as we three caught the dripping cream before it ran down the sides of the cone onto our hands.

Precious loves vanilla ice cream. She sat on my lap and licked while I turned the cone and wiped the sticky drips. Tourists gathered around and watched her devour the treat.

An older woman in a wheelchair came over to us. Her daughter spoke. "I never knew cats liked ice cream. And, look, Mother, she walks on a leash!" The young woman stared in amazement.

"Mother loves cats. She misses hers. She has three at home but couldn't bring them with her. May she pet your cat?" she asked.

I put Precious on the woman's lap in the wheelchair. The old lady's eyes sparkled. "Oh kitty. You're so soft and beautiful. Just precious. What's her name?"

"Precious," I responded.

"That's obvious, but what's her name?"

"That *is* her name. Precious," I chuckled.

"How appropriate," she remarked as she stroked the cat's long silky fur. The sight-seeing boat was secured at the gang plank, discharging passengers. The daughter of the woman holding the cat bent down in front of her mother. "Won't you change your mind and go on the river tour? It's perfectly safe. I don't want to go without you."

Mother shook her head. "No. I'm afraid of boats. You and Dave go. I'll stay here with the cat. We'll be just fine, won't we, Precious?"

"But Mother, maybe these ladies and Precious have

other plans. Besides, I bet Precious wouldn't be afraid of riding on a boat."

"Probably not," the older woman responded. She looked my way. "You wouldn't want to go on a boat ride, would you?"

Her daughter was mortified. "Mother!" she wailed.

"Well, I thought if Precious went, so would I." Muriel and I looked at each other, then glanced at the disabled woman cuddling the cat. We shrugged our shoulders. In unison we blurted, "Why not?"

Precious stayed on her friend's lap as Dave, the son-in-law, maneuvered the wheelchair down the gangplank. Both occupants of the chair bounced with the movement of the wheels going over the cleats on the walkway.

The ticket taker looked at the pair, smiled and commented, "We usually don't allow pets on these vessels, but since you two are so content and the cat has a leash, she must be well trained. I'll let you on. Enjoy your ride."

The wheelchair was rolled out to the bow of the vessel and secured. The riverboat guide began his narration. "Over to your right is the famous Pirate's Cove..." Precious and Mrs. Wheeler stretched their necks to observe the sight. "On your left are Navy Dry Docks." Again the necks stretched.

Before long a group had gathered around the pair. All admired the cat and sang praises to the old woman for having such a well-behaved pet. Everyone talked, laughed and had a great time. The cat enjoyed all the attention. Hardly anyone in the immediate area paid much attention to the tour guide's voice. They were all too busy exchanging pet tales. The daughter of Mrs. Wheeler, our wheelchair friend, joined us.

"I haven't seen Mother so happy in a week," she said. "We thought this trip might be good for her. She hasn't been anywhere since her stroke. But she has done nothing but worry about her cats. Precious is adorable."

We all chuckled as we watched this remarkable feline. "She's such a ham. Thanks for going along on this boat ride. I know you changed your plans to do so." (I don't think we really had a choice. This feline pretty much governs her own time and activity.) "Precious has most certainly made our day," the young woman remarked as cameras clicked, and we all bade farewell to go our separate ways.

As always, Precious made our day, too. She also made us miss the last tram back to our motel. We had to call a cab. When we opened the door to our room, the cat headed straight for her litter pan. Five hours of touring, boating and being manhandled must have raised havoc with her kidneys.

Precious doesn't care if she crashes a domestic meeting or has encounters in foreign countries. She's at home wherever she sets her feet down. On our way to Nova Scotia we were informed that the ship going across the lower end of the Province wouldn't allow us to keep the cat with us. Precious would have to be put in the cargo area.

We would not do that. This meant taking the highway the long way around up through New Brunswick and over to the upper section of Nova Scotia. That was OK with us.

The customs officer was in his guard house, all decked out in his fancy uniform. Precious was hanging over the top of the back seat, sound asleep. The officer looked in the back of the station wagon and remarked, "What a beautiful lifelike stuffed animal." I said nothing as I reached back to get Precious's papers from her luggage. Just as I handed the certificates to the Canadian, the car in back of us backfired. Startled by the noise, Precious fell from her perch and scurried to the front seat.

The officer jumped back and yelled, "My God. It's alive!" He turned white as a ghost. He never did look at her papers or stamp them. Because the papers had not been fully documented, we half expected a mounty to come up behind us and pull us over to confiscate our most prized possession—Precious. However, the trip was uneventful until we reached the Nova Scotia border.

As we entered this province, there was a huge sign, "Welcome to Nova Scotia." The area looked like a small park with grass, trees and shrubs. Shops and rest rooms lined the sides. We pulled into the curb and got out.

After using the restrooms and browsing through the shops, we walked out onto the green. Under the welcome sign was a Scotsman in full dress parading back and forth playing the bagpipes. Children followed the bagpiper while tourists strolled around the green.

Precious pulled toward the musician in kilts. She managed to catch the attention of the entertainer. He stopped, bent down and scratched her ears. The bagpipes once again wailed their eerie sound.

The cat tugged to follow. Muriel unleashed her. Precious bounded over to join the march. The Scotsman marched—the cat marched. The man in kilts stopped. So did the cat. Soon there was a crowd, all laughing at the seriousness of the exhibitors. One woman remarked, "This is better than the ducks down south parading to their water at the hotel."

(We had been there but were not allowed anywhere near the feathered bathers. We were told, *"No pets allowed,"* for safety purposes. I still say they were afraid the cat would upstage those quackers.

They get no plug from me. I'm not naming the hotel.)

We think Precious thought the bagpipe player was our neighbor who plays the bagpipes. He practices outside because his wife won't let him make that noise in the house. Can't say I blame her. It's hard enough living a few doors down the street.

Together Muriel, Precious and I have traveled thousands of miles—from Nova Scotia to Florida—to the Mississippi River and everywhere in between.

We have watched the sun rise over the Atlantic Ocean as we strolled the sandy beaches in Florida. Precious chased waves as they pushed against the shore while my eyes searched the horizon.

We've also seen the sun say good night behind the majestic pines in Maine. We sat on a bench, two big, yellow eyes—two blue and two brown eyes staring at the magnificent shades of pink, red, orange and blue painted across the sky. We lingered, the cat with her old red jacket, Muriel and me with sweaters, as the moon peeked over the hill. As if for our pleasure alone, night creatures began their symphony which continued into the darkness. A cool breeze skipped past us leaving the scent of pine needles and wild flowers trailing behind.

We have worked our way through stifling heat in the Alabama flats to ice storms in the West Virginia Mountains. We have shared ice cream cones and steak in almost every state we visited. Big yellow eyes, another pair colored brown, taking in the splendors of Mother Nature from the Blue Ridge Mountains to the jagged Maritime coastline, my faithful fur-covered companion putting complete trust in the person behind the wheel in the car.

There hasn't been much traveling or visiting these past fifteen months. Precious has been losing her balance and falling from her favorite places. X-rays show the metal pins in her hind legs have shifted. Occasionally she extends a muted cry but never complains.

However, manhandling takes a lot out of her. We no longer cut grass or work on inlaid pictures. While I pound typewriter keys the typing critic basks in the sun on the window sill.

February of this year, while I was typing, I heard a loud thud. I went into the living room and found my furry friend in a heap on the floor. She had fallen from her wood box. She didn't move when I picked her up. I thought she was dead. I rubbed her head, legs and stomach. After a few minutes she rallied, almost as if coming out of a faint.

Extensive blood tests showed serious kidney and liver ailments. She also had a fever. Antibiotics took care of the fever. Dr. White gave me capsules which had to be administered every day. The pills were gigantic. A cow would have trouble swallowing them. We had to remove the dry powder from the capsule, mix it with a little water in a shot glass and put it into an eye dropper.

The medicine made her up-chuck. It's no wonder if it tasted anything like it smelled. I couldn't get the odor off my hands even after numerous scrubbings. Precious had no appetite. We spent much of our day and night sitting and rocking. I thought, "Dear God, don't tell me it's going to end as it all began so many years ago."

The cat lost weight. Her eyes were cloudy. She wanted to be held most of the time. Every hour or so I tried to push nourishment into her thin body. I saw no sense in forcing her to take medication that continually made her sick to her stomach. If my friend was going to die, let her pass away without the agony of constantly being nauseated. The doctor agreed.

News of Precious's illness spread quickly. Telephone calls and cards poured in from all over the eastern part of the country. I spent most of my free time writing notes of thanks and reporting on our friend's condition. To save time we had address labels imprinted with her name. No cards came from the goose at Ann Lee Pond or the German Shepherd, but many inquiries did arrive from other fur-covered friends.

Gradually, she took more and more nourishment. When she returned to the doctor's office, Dr. White couldn't believe his eyes. He took more tests. He thought he had made a mistake. The cat's condition had improved to almost normal. Unbelievable! The tests confirmed that Precious was bouncing back to her old self. Eating improved. It seemed she had four hollow legs. I couldn't fill her up, feeding her dime-sized pieces of ground round—one piece at a time. I would have spent all day feeding her, if that would make the difference.

It was obvious she felt better. She was bored. This feline wanted to *go*, but we stayed around the house. Muriel kept her occupied while I returned to my typewriter.

Her latest doctor's visit showed Precious's condition declining again, but not to the extent it was originally. But—the smelly medicine must once again be consumed. This time the dosage was half a pill instead of the full one. She kept this down.

Precious knows she must have breakfast and take her medicine before she can go outside for the day. One day she refused to take it. We had words. She went into her bedroom and refused to come out. If she couldn't go outside, forget it. She curled up on her cushion.

I thought I might fool her by mixing the medicine in some juice from her canned food. I set the dish down in front of her. She smelled, licked a few times and walked away towards the outside door.

"You can't go out until you at least finish the juice on your food!" I warned her. A few more swipes at the food and back to the door. "I said *all* the juice."

"Iiow, iow."

"Yes, I love you, too, but that is not going to let you off the hook. You can't go out until you finish this." I pushed the dish closer to her. More pacing. Precious knew I meant business. She marched around the dish several times before she stopped and took a lick.

"All of it," I scolded. She went to the dish and sucked up some liquid. I stirred. She licked. Soon the food that remained was bone dry. The cat looked up at me with those big yellow eyes that said, "There. Now can I go out?" What's a body to do? Out she went. A promise is a promise. The eye dropper was put into use again.

Once more we were inundated with cards and phone calls. The only call Precious will take is from my sister Helen in Florida. This cat senses when Aunt Helen is on the telephone. If she's inside, she comes over to me, I put her on my lap and hold the telephone receiver to the cat's ear. Helen talks—Precious listens. I believe this cat understands every word she hears.

Not long after I completed the manuscript for this book, Muriel and I took a five-hour trip to a nursing home in New Hampshire to visit a friend of ours.

The motel where we usually stay had heating problems, and they couldn't accommodate us. The other two motels in town wouldn't take pets. The motel manager where we had made reservations called a friend who operated a resort just out of town. The "Inn" wouldn't take us because of the cat, but they had a group of timeshare buildings that were available. We had an entire building to ourselves that night.

During the night it snowed eight inches, and it was still coming down when we got up the next morning. No way would we start out for our return trip in the snowstorm. Muriel went to the office to book us for another night. She was told we would have to move from that building because they were expecting a party from Massachusetts, and all twenty-four rooms were taken. No problem; we moved into the building next door.

That night I had to make a telephone call. There was no telephone in the building where we were staying, but I knew there was a pay telephone in the building we had vacated that morning. I trudged through the snow, stepped inside and saw eighteen people standing and sitting around in the hall. One man was on the phone.

"Is everyone waiting to use the telephone?" I asked. No, I was told. The people gathered there were part of the "party." While waiting I started up a conversation with one of the women sitting in the lounge.

Every year, I learned, the family reserves this building for their Christmas party. About one hundred family members attend. Each room is an efficiency apartment that sleeps six. There is an adjoining swimming pool and a recreation hall, a beautiful setup. They all arrive on Friday night, go out and chop Christmas trees Saturday morning and then ski or go on sleigh rides. Saturday night each family brings a casserole to the recreation hall where they have dinner, sing, dance, exchange gifts and play games.

About then a young mother carried her infant daughter up the hall. The baby was crying her lungs out. Apparently she had a cat at home and always went to sleep with the cat in her crib. Her mother and father had forgotten to put a stuffed cat into the bag when they packed, and the kid was howling.

"I'm going into town to see if I can buy a stuffed toy," the father said.

Who was he kidding? I thought. In this town they pull the sidewalks in at 6 p.m. There was only one store that sold stuffed animals, and it was closed. I told him so.

I should have minded my own business and made my exit after my telephone call, but I couldn't bear hearing this baby crying like that. No, I had to go over to the woman and child. She didn't know what she was going to do.

"Do you think the baby will eventually settle down?" I asked.

"No," was the quick answer. "She'll have us up all night."

I opened my mouth. "I have a cat," I heard myself say. "I'll be glad to get her if it will help."

The instant the little girl saw Precious she stopped crying and reached for the cat's head. In two minutes she was fast asleep.

Muriel had come to the building with me on my return with Precious, and we were asked to join the party in full swing in the recreation hall. We mingled with the group for a while, but we left because we wanted to start out early the next morning. Unfortunately, it snowed still more that night, so we had to stay another night.

Saturday morning the tree choppers headed off into the woods. The baby girl was looking for her furry friend. Precious was in the middle of everything.

She even went sleigh riding with the baby in a plastic sleigh, her red jacket wrapped around her and a car robe tucked in around the child and the cat. Muriel and I helped the children make snowmen and build snow forts for a snowball fight.

When I picked up Precious so we could go to town to eat, we were invited to join the party for their gala spread.

"We couldn't do that," we demurred.

"Why not?" one woman asked. "Precious has been babysitting since last night."

I pointed to the sign, "NO PETS ALLOWED" on the door to the recreation hall. One of the boys took the sign off the wall. Precious was the life of the party. She helped unwrapped gifts, rummaged through the discarded wrappings, and even helped decorate the tree. She almost fell into the swimming pool. The piano and organ player broke his glasses, and no one else was musically inclined, so Muriel gave in and continued with musical numbers on the organ.

Precious curled up with the baby in the baby carrier, lying almost on top of the youngster. About then the resort manager walked by with several bottles of wine and soda. He saw the cat and said, "Sorry. The cat isn't allowed in here."

The mother spoke up. "That's not a cat," she said. "She's been babysitting since last night." The manager shook his head, wished everyone a happy holiday and left.

The following morning a crowd gathered outside our room singing Christmas carols. Someone had packed a "CARE" package for our long trip home. As we drove away the countryside looked like a Currier and Ives painting. Youngsters chased after the car yelling, "Write to us, Precious!" "Safe trip home!"

What a joy it was seeing all those family members having a good time. No fights. No harsh words. Just having fun. In my family we aren't together for an hour and someone starts a fight.

Muriel was tired by the time we got home from driving on such slippery roads, but Precious was gloating over the great time she'd had. I caught a miserable cold and ended up with an extra fifty Christmas cards to address to our new friends.

I know I'm going to miss all of this when Precious finally reaches the end of her days. She's already lived the equivalent of about a hundred human years, and I know she can't live forever.

Our immediate plans are uncertain because of Precious's health. If she is physically able and so desires, we would like to make at least one more trip with her. What better way to end a career in social services than to visit where it all began years ago— Aunt B's nursing home in Pennsylvania! And what better way to remember the good old days when she was a drill sergeant than to visit Gettysburg where one of the most deadly battles was fought between the states!

The cat will be allowed to take the riding tour. After that, other members of our party will do house-to-house tours. Precious and I will go any place she chooses to take me. I'm sure there will be a crowd gathered wherever she decides to wander.

I can't help but wonder what would have happened during that great war if the drill sergeant had lived back then. I can hear her loud and clear as both sides prepared to do battle. "ERRO. ERRO!" Both the blue and gray would have snapped to attention in short order.

If she feels up to it, we will go on other adventures. Who knows? I might be able to gather enough information for *Simply Precious II...*

Should she be unable to go on any more trips or adventures, I will be content to stay home and be with her. There are many places I'd like to visit, but they will have to wait. My companion's well-being is more important to me.

It wouldn't be the same without her. There would be no limelight, no crowds following us, no talking with complete strangers without cause, no more anxiety attacks from not knowing what will happen next.

The time Precious and I have left together is special to both of us. She continues to follow me everywhere I go and continues to wait outside the bathroom door for both Muriel and me. Even though she is in poor health she continues to watch over both of us when we are sick, just as the two of us drop everything when she requires any kind of attention. Each of us knows we are there for each other, no matter what. Now, instead of bounding into the middle of crafts on the snack tray, Precious eats from a tray. We have our evening meal in the living room while we watch the news, "Wheel of Fortune" and "Jeopardy." I bring her onto my lap after dinner and brush her while Muriel washes the dishes. Before bedtime, both cat and Muriel have a snack. After "Night Line" the TV is turned off. The cat jumps from my lap, goes to the bathroom door and waits for me to come out. She then hitches a ride on my shoulder to her bedroom. We always end our day as we begin it—with a hug, a kiss, an "iow" and "I love you, too."

Nights when I'm unable to sleep, Precious joins me in the rocking chair to read. The book rests against her body as I stroke her ears and rock back and forth. On those sleepless nights we continue to have our bowls of Rice Krispies. While we eat and read I think about our nights together on top of our mountain many years ago.

On cold winter days we continue to view nature through the picture window from our rocking chair. We watch the birds and squirrels go to and fro from the feeders hanging on the Douglas fir tree by the garage, remembering our beaver, bear and bird friends from years gone by and the many happy hours we spent on the snow-covered fields. Those moments were ours alone.

On warmer days we sit on our bench under the old maple tree soaking up the late day's sunshine while watching fabulous sunsets just like those we saw in Maine. Two loyal old friends—me wearing a heavier sweater than I did years ago, Precious with her old red jacket—sharing many happy memories of love, companionship and trust while thanking God for His very special gift to each of us.

A TRIBUTE TO PRECIOUS

I had survived for over fifty-five years, living what I felt was a good and complete life. I had my health, a good job, friends, offered a helping hand to those less fortunate than I, respected nature and all living things.

Little did I realize when I picked you up from under that porch chair in 1980, my life would never again be the same. Not only did you become my best friend, you became my teacher—my mentor. You first showed me how every living creature fights to survive. The days and weeks I held, nursed, comforted and protected you, you fought with every breath within you to survive. It was so hard for you to eat and take your medication. You put your complete trust in me, as a friend, and never gave up.

A sampler picture hangs in my hallway. It reads, "All that we send into the lives of others comes back into our own." I never dreamed this applied to animals, but you proved me wrong. Through the years, it has

---

been *you* who has given so much of yourself for the happiness of others.

Those painful days and agonizing nights that both Muriel and I spent with our aching broken twisted limbs, were made more bearable by your being there with every move we made. Without regard for your own well-being, you stood guard, watching over each of us.

Your keen perception taught us to look beyond the surface and into the hearts of those who share our planet. You gave new meaning to life for lonely shut-ins. Many had given up on themselves until you began to visit them. You showed them how important they are to you by letting them hug, kiss and rock you on their laps. Sometimes you, yourself, were in pain from your own ailments. You taught us how important it is to remember people confined to nursing homes. The expressions of joy on their faces when you walked down those corridors and into their rooms are worth thousands of words.

Another lesson I learned was how important it is to have a friend near when a person is about to die. The last thing on Kevin Babcock's mind was his friend, Precious. You were with him to the end. He loved you so much. The peaceful look on the boy's face told his mother he was happy.

Since you came to live with me, I look at everything in a different light. Instead of zooming down the highway, eyes glued to the road, signs or pavement, I now take time to look at the world around me.

We've stopped to gather rocks for our rock garden, helped a turtle on his journey across a highway, picked weeds with blossoms choked with road dust.

Waves from the Atlantic Ocean mystified us as they raced to shore—you chasing them as they rolled against the sandy beach. Sea gulls joined in on your chase, but all in vain, as the foamy white liquid rapidly receded to join the massive body of water from where it came. I never fully understood the part tides play in our universe until I watched you, the gulls and the tide playing tag at the shoreline. It made me curious to read more about it.

Sitting in the quiet of early evening on a bench in Maine nudged my memory of times spent on our mountain—just you and me. It aroused my awareness that there is beauty even in silence and darkness.

Thanks to you, we saw Savannah from the riverboat. The new bridge, over the river, stood like magnified string art with large shiny cables reaching for the sky, forming the illusion of a giant merchant sailing ship, anchor dropped, protecting the harbor. It took everyone's breath away. Even you stretched your neck and turned your eyes upward as we chugged beneath this incredible structure. We wouldn't have gone on that boat trip had you not made friends with Mrs. Wheeler, your wheelchair buddy.

You knew long before we did when Muriel's father and my two sisters died in 1982, 1993 and 1995. You comforted us and told us everything was all right. You were there for us and understood our loss, You showed the same compassion when Snowshoes died, this time letting us know animals mourn too. And we were there for you.

You've opened my eyes to the intricacies of life around me. How to take time out from my busy schedule to stop and explore nature's wonders. You helped teach me understanding and patience.

Because of you, we sat perfectly still for hours, watched wild life go about their business of living, while human work went unattended. You taught me how to understand myself, how to enjoy life while making this a better, happier more compassionate world to live in.

There must be an invisible magnet within you as

Simply Precious

you draw a crowd wherever you go. I didn't object to most of these incidents, but I never would have stopped and witnessed the bagpipe playing Scotsman in Nova Scotia. You insisted. As always, you were in the limelight, Muriel and me standing in your shadow.

DEAR FRIEND—I would be both honored and proud to walk anywhere in the shadow of your little five-pound fur-covered body—for I know it would lead me to some exciting adventure or teach me yet another lesson about life.

For all you are and have been for all these many years, sharing these Precious moments in time, I am eternally grateful. You ARE remarkable.

SIMPLY PRECIOUS.